VOLUME 19

OLD TESTAMENT

THE NEW COLLEGEVILLE BIBLE COMMENTARY

JOB

Kathleen M. O'Connor

SERIES EDITOR

Daniel Durken, O.S.B.

LITURGICAL PRESS

Collegeville, Minnesota

www.litpress.org

Nihil Obstat: Reverend Robert Harren, *Censor deputatus*.
Imprimatur: ✠ Most Reverend John F. Kinney, J.C.D., D.D., Bishop of St. Cloud, Minnesota, October 12, 2012.

Design by Ann Blattner.

Cover illustration: Detail of Job *Frontispiece* by Donald Jackson. © 2007 *The Saint John's Bible*, Order of Saint Benedict, Collegeville, Minnesota, USA. Used with permission. All rights reserved.

Photos: page 14, Hugh Witzmann, O.S.B.; page 21, Wikimedia Commons; pages 70, 87, and 94, Thinkstock Photos.

1   2   3   4   5   6   7   8   9

Library of Congress Cataloging-in-Publication Data

O'Connor, Kathleen M., 1942–
    Job / Kathleen M. O'Connor.
        p. cm. — (New Collegeville Bible commentary. Old Testament ; v. 19)
    ISBN 978-0-8146-2853-9
    1. Bible. O.T. Job.—Commentaries.   I. Title.

BS1415.53.O26   2012
223'.1077—dc23

2012031414

CONTENTS

ABBREVIATIONS

Books of the Bible

Acts—Acts of the Apostles
Amos—Amos
Bar—Baruch
1 Chr—1 Chronicles
2 Chr—2 Chronicles
Col—Colossians
1 Cor—1 Corinthians
2 Cor—2 Corinthians
Dan—Daniel
Deut—Deuteronomy
Eccl (or Qoh)—Ecclesiastes
Eph—Ephesians
Esth—Esther
Exod—Exodus
Ezek—Ezekiel
Ezra—Ezra
Gal—Galatians
Gen—Genesis
Hab—Habakkuk
Hag—Haggai
Heb—Hebrews
Hos—Hosea
Isa—Isaiah
Jas—James
Jdt—Judith
Jer—Jeremiah
Job—Job
Joel—Joel
John—John
1 John—1 John
2 John—2 John
3 John—3 John
Jonah—Jonah
Josh—Joshua
Jude—Jude
Judg—Judges
1 Kgs—1 Kings

2 Kgs—2 Kings
Lam—Lamentations
Lev—Leviticus
Luke—Luke
1 Macc—1 Maccabees
2 Macc—2 Maccabees
Mal—Malachi
Mark—Mark
Matt—Matthew
Mic—Micah
Nah—Nahum
Neh—Nehemiah
Num—Numbers
Obad—Obadiah
1 Pet—1 Peter
2 Pet—2 Peter
Phil—Philippians
Phlm—Philemon
Prov—Proverbs
Ps(s)—Psalms
Rev—Revelation
Rom—Romans
Ruth—Ruth
1 Sam—1 Samuel
2 Sam—2 Samuel
Sir—Sirach
Song—Song of Songs
1 Thess—1 Thessalonians
2 Thess—2 Thessalonians
1 Tim—1 Timothy
2 Tim—2 Timothy
Titus—Titus
Tob—Tobit
Wis—Wisdom
Zech—Zechariah
Zeph—Zephaniah

The Book of Job

The book of Job is vivid testimony to pain, a plea for justice, and a wrenching theological debate about suffering and its causes. Central to this debate are questions about the roles God and humans play in causing human suffering and whether divine-human relationship can proceed in the midst of overwhelming anguish. Like a riddle, the text grasps readers' minds and emotions, inviting them to participate in Job's story and to work toward their own solution to the dilemmas of both Job and his friends.

Literary features

The book's literary components do not fit easily together. It sets conflicting characters and discordant speeches side by side without providing interpretive clues. But rather than producing a mish-mash of ideas, the resulting tensions summon readers to engage in Job's struggle, to stay with him on the ash heap and stand with him before God in search of healing. Because the book refuses to leave our present understandings intact, reading means undertaking mental and emotional labor. Job and his friends argue with each other in dense, beautiful poetic speeches, and they complain at length to wear the reader down. In the process, the poems bring us into Job's despair and his friends' frustration and growing rigidity.

But the effort required to read and study the book is worth it because the book's unsettled nature puts us either in Job's place or in sympathy with his friends or, perhaps, both. Precisely because it refuses to settle for easy answers about any of its subjects, the book of Job is a classic of world literature.

Most interpreters believe the book as we now have it is a composite, built upon an ancient tale about an innocent sufferer. The outlines of Job's story were well known across cultures in antiquity. Peoples of the ancient Near East produced several texts with affinities to the biblical book where an innocent person undergoes suffering, argues with the gods, and is inexplicably restored to well-being. Job also appears by name in a biblical list of heroes (Ezek 14:14, 20), adding to the sense that his basic story was widely known.

It is likely that a writer in ancient Israel took this folktale, adapted it, cut it open, and then set the poetic speeches in the midst of it. The prose narrative appears in the prologue (1:1–2:13) and epilogue (42:7-17). By using both forms of literature, folktale and poetry, the book presents a totality of suffering, an overwhelming portrait told from outside by a third person narrator in the prose and from the inside in the poetic testimony of Job and his friends. The prose describes Job's external losses, while the poetry portrays Job's more internal sufferings.

Poetry is particularly suited to the task of spiritual struggle because its dense imagery, compactness of speech, and allusiveness create an artistic world something like music. It appeals to the full humanity of readers, summoning forth our own ghosts, unsettled sorrows, and hidden angers. It can transport us into realms of spirit and lead to new discoveries. But the poetry of Job makes best sense when read in the context of the prose narrative that lays out the book's initial problem. Job is an innocent person yet enormous catastrophes befall him because of a deal made in heaven. This predicament gives rise to the poetry.

The prose and the poetry belong together, but there are great differences between them. In the prologue, for example, Job is patient and trusting while his friends are silent. By contrast, in the poetry Job is furious and impatient and his friends flood him with words. This is one of the many gaps that raise questions about characters and their motivations, thereby engaging us in Job's plight.

Job's poetry uses a great deal of legal imagery as a way for Job to imagine that God might acknowledge his innocence. Job appeals to a third party to assist him in his search for justice because his informal appeals to God seem to produce nothing but more sorrow. He declares legal oaths of innocence by which he offers his self-defense at the end of his speeches. But legal language is only one way Job voices his complaints. Language of creation and observations from the world of plants and animals help him build his protests.

Much of Job's speech takes the form of lamentation. Over one third of the book of Psalms and the entire book of Lamentations are laments. These are prayers in the form of complaint. The one who prays cries out to God in pain, describes various forms of affliction, and seeks redress. Laments are a form of truth-telling to God. They open up rather than deny suffering, and they present to God the affliction of the one who prays and demands action. In Old Testament laments, anger at God and fury close to blasphemy are instruments of fidelity because they keep the relationship with God alive in the midst of suffering. They are acts of faith that God cares for the afflicted and can bear to hear the truth. By using laments, Job grows strong and courageous as he clings to God under the worst conditions.

Wisdom literature

The book of Job belongs in a grouping of biblical books called the wisdom literature that includes Proverbs, Ecclesiastes, Sirach, and the Wisdom of Solomon. These books differ from other biblical literature in their attention to daily struggles of ordinary human life. By contrast, the prophetic books speak of God's word to the people, and the historical books tell of God's actions on behalf of Israel. Wisdom starts neither with God nor with large political and national events, but from human efforts to live wisely from day to day. Life's challenges give rise to theological reflection, not the other way around. Job is merely going on with his daily life when disasters overtake him, and those events propel his theological questions. In wisdom thinking, at least in the book of Proverbs, faithful living should yield material blessing. When Job loses everything, his fidelity to God is suspect.

Job's cultural world

Job lived in a different cultural world from that of contemporary Western readers, though people in tribal communities on various continents may find many affinities with aspects of the book. Job lived in a community-oriented culture. The family and clan were of high value, and one sought to become wise and learn proverbs in order to create harmony for in the community, not for self-advancement as in individual-oriented cultures.

Israel's culture as reflected in Wisdom literature was deeply concerned about the authenticity of speech, about proper use of the tongue, and about wise sayings or proverbs as a key to right behavior. Proverbs are short sayings that were instruments of wise living and the storehouse of tradition. Because the culture was an oral one, the right use of words was critical for communal well-being. Wisdom drawn from animal and plant life instructed humans in how to maneuver in daily life and how to contribute to the community. Both Job and his friends apply proverbs to his situation, but their proverbs usually conflict with one another.

Other features of Israel's culture important for understanding the book include the values of honor and shame. Shame was a communal judgment, often implicit, that one's behavior or attitude brought dishonor to the community. To be shamed means one has been disrespectful of persons or basic values in the community. Job begins the story as a most honorable person, but his disasters cause him shame and isolation from his friends. He loses his good name and his community no longer recognizes his honor, isolating him and causing him great anguish. Many Asian and African cultures structure themselves with similar values.

Outline of the book

The book divides into the following literary units:

The Prologue (1:1–2:13)

Three Rounds of Speeches among Job and His Friends
  (3:1–14:22; 15:1–21:34; 22:1–31:37)

Hymn to Wisdom (28:1-28)

Job's Self-Defense (29:1–31:37)

Elihu's Speech (32:1–37:24)

The Encounter with God in the Storm (38:1–42:6)

The Epilogue (42:7-17)

The Book of Job

I. Prologue

Job's Piety. ¹In the land of Uz there was a blameless and upright man named Job, who feared God and avoided evil. ²Seven sons and three daughters were born to him; ³and he had seven thousand sheep, three thousand camels, five hundred yoke of oxen, five hundred she-donkeys, and a very large household, so that he was greater than anyone in the East. ⁴His sons used to take turns giving feasts, sending invitations to their three sisters to eat and drink with them. ⁵And when each feast had run its course, ▸ Job would send for them and sanctify them, rising early and offering sacrifices for every one of them. For Job said, "It may be that my children have sinned and cursed God in their hearts." Job did this habitually.

The Interview Between the Lord and the Satan. ⁶One day, when the sons ▸

PROLOGUE

Job 1:1–2:3

The prose prologue begins with a depiction of a contented Job, residing in security, wealth, and domestic tranquility. A narrator describes events that move through the slow but complete unraveling of these good things and end in grief on the ash heap. Events alternate in the five scenes between earth and heaven; events in heaven determine what happens on earth. The narrative unfolds in highly stylized fashion with sparse detail and repeated patterns typical of a folktale. The effects of this narrative style are to present a hammering sequence of events that shatters Job's world and leaves many unanswered questions about divine and human characters and their motivations.

1:1-5 Job's goodness

The opening scene takes place on earth where every detail contributes to a portrait of Job as innocent man, beloved of God. The narrator calls him

▸ This symbol indicates a cross reference number in the *Catechism of the Catholic Church.* See page 109 for number citations.

of God came to present themselves before the LORD, the satan also came among them. [7]The LORD said to the satan, "Where have you been?" Then the satan answered the LORD and said, "Roaming the earth and patrolling it." [8]The LORD said to the satan, "Have you noticed my servant Job? There is no one on earth like him, blameless and upright, fearing God and avoiding evil." [9]The satan answered the LORD and said, "Is it for nothing that Job is God-fearing? [10]Have you not surrounded him and his family and all that he has with your protection? You have blessed the work of his hands, and his livestock are spread over the land. [11]But now put forth your hand and touch all that he has, and surely he will curse you to your face." [12]The LORD said to the satan, "Very well, all that he has is in your

---

"blameless and upright," one who "feared God," and "avoided evil" (1:1). To "fear God" is a common term of the wisdom literature that has less to do with fright before God and more to do with right relationship with God. "Fear of God" is not easy to translate into English but conveys qualities of obedience, reverence, and awe before God. One commentator calls it a synonym for true religion. Job's fear of God marks him as a wise and righteous man. His large family and vast wealth in animal holdings confirm his blamelessness and special relationship with God. In antiquity, material wealth signified that its bearer was a worthy recipient of divine favor.

Job's uprightness receives further confirmation from the size of his family and the peaceful generosity of his children. His seven sons invite his three daughters to their feasts, showing their hospitality to exceed the bounds of their culture where women had little status. And perhaps most indicative of Job's righteousness is a detail in which he exceeds all obvious requirements of care for his family by offering sacrifice on behalf of his children in case they have sinned "in their hearts" (1:5). In its spare telling, the story leaves readers to ponder Job's behavior. Is he an overly scrupulous parent? Does he act to protect the children? Or is this one more instance of his absolute devotion to God? The folktale genre of the prologue, however, may preclude suspicions about Job's character, for folktales typically tell actions as straightforward events to be taken at face value. The next scenes support the view that fidelity alone motivates Job.

1:6-12 Deal in heaven

The action starts when messengers, called "sons of God," come before "the LORD" in the heavenly court. Heavenly courts with semi-divine beings of the spirit world appear elsewhere in the Old Testament (1 Kgs 22:19-23; Dan 7). Among the heavenly messengers is "the Satan," whose name means "the adversary," an official court title, not a proper name. He is not yet the demonic figure of later Jewish and Christian thinking, but one of the Lord's

power; only do not lay a hand on him." So the satan went forth from the presence of the LORD.

The First Trial. ¹³One day, while his sons and daughters were eating and drinking wine in the house of their eldest brother, ¹⁴a messenger came to Job and said, "The oxen were plowing and the donkeys grazing beside them, ¹⁵and the Sabeans carried them off in a raid. They put the servants to the sword, and I alone have escaped to tell you." ¹⁶He was still speaking when another came and said,

"God's fire has fallen from heaven and struck the sheep and the servants and consumed them; I alone have escaped to tell you." ¹⁷He was still speaking when another came and said, "The Chaldeans formed three columns, seized the camels, carried them off, and put the servants to the sword; I alone have escaped to tell you." ¹⁸He was still speaking when another came and said, "Your sons and daughters were eating and drinking wine in the house of their eldest brother, ¹⁹and suddenly a great wind came from

faithful servants, though it is easy to see from his role here how he might later come to personify evil.

The Lord starts the action by asking the Satan if, when traveling to and fro on the earth, he had noticed "my servant Job" (1:7). Should readers still question Job's innocence, God's authoritative boasting repeats the narrator's assessment of Job's innocence. Job is "blameless and upright, fearing God and avoiding evil" (1:8). The Satan, however, suspects Job is faithful only because God has given him good things. He accuses God of purchasing Job's fidelity, for if God were to remove them, "surely [Job] will curse you to your face" (1:11). The Hebrew word translated "curse" means literally "to bless," but here "bless" is a euphemism, that is, a polite way to say the opposite.

Without hesitation and without debate, the Lord gives the Satan control of Job's life with one caveat—he is not to touch Job. Why God acquiesces to this deal is not clear. It may be that refusing the Satan's challenge would cause God shame in this ancient Israelite culture where honor is of high value. Or it may be that God is so confident of Job's loyalty that a positive outcome of the deal seems assured. Whatever God's reasons for abdicating power, Satan goes forth to loose tragedy upon Job.

1:13-22 Job's first test

Back on earth, catastrophes roll over Job in quick succession. In simple, unadorned prose, the story unfolds in parallel episodes so each disaster appears like the one before in a persistent drumbeat of loss. Events concerning Job's children form a literary frame around his other losses (1:13, 18-19). By setting the other disasters during one of their feasts, the text creates a foreboding sense of doom and foreshadows the fourth and most horrible

across the desert and smashed the four corners of the house. It fell upon the young people and they are dead; I alone have escaped to tell you."

Job's Reaction. [20]Then Job arose and tore his cloak and cut off his hair. He fell to the ground and worshiped. [21]He said,

> "Naked I came forth from my
>   mother's womb,
>   and naked shall I go back there.
> The LORD gave and the LORD has
>   taken away;
>   blessed be the name of the
>   LORD!"

[22]In all this Job did not sin, nor did he charge God with wrong.

2 **The Second Interview.** [1]One day, when the sons of God came to present themselves before the LORD, the satan also came with them. [2]The LORD said to the satan, "Where have you been?" Then the satan answered the LORD and said, "Roaming the earth and patrolling it." [3]The LORD said to the satan, "Have you noticed my servant Job? There is no one on earth like him, blameless and upright, fearing God and avoiding evil. He still holds fast to his innocence although you incited me against him to ruin him for nothing." [4]The satan answered the LORD and said, "Skin for skin! All that a man has he will give for his life. [5]But put forth your hand and touch his bone and his flesh. Then surely he will curse you to your face." [6]And the LORD said to the satan, "He is in your power; only spare his life."

---

of Job's devastations. A messenger comes to announce each tragedy and says, "I alone have escaped to tell you" (1:15, 16, 17, 18). And "He was still speaking when" the next messenger appears with a similar report. Finally, in the horrible climax, the narrator gives extra description to the children's destruction. A great wind destroys the house where they are feasting and kills all of them. Within a few verses, Job loses everything in a whirlwind of calamity, a blitz of overwhelmingly bad news.

To this point in the telling, Job has made no response to any of the reports, but then in customary rituals for expressing grief, he tears his clothes, cuts his hair, and falls upon the ground. At last he speaks in carefully balanced sentences typical of Hebrew poetry. "Naked I came forth . . . naked shall I go back . . . The LORD gave . . . the LORD has taken away" (1:21). Then he blesses God's name. Job does not curse God and the narrator confirms that Job does not "sin, nor did he charge God with wrong" (1:22).

2:1-6 Another bad deal in heaven

The story might have ended in the previous chapter where, even in the aftermath of the unrelenting assault upon him, Job proved himself blameless and upright, a God-fearer, and a refuser of evil. Instead, when the heavenly messengers come before the Lord again, the tension escalates. The narrative follows the first heavenly scene of the previous chapter, but with some important changes. Again God asks the Satan where he has been

The Second Trial. ⁷So the satan went forth from the presence of the LORD and struck Job with severe boils from the soles of his feet to the crown of his head.

Job's Reaction. ⁸He took a potsherd to scrape himself, as he sat among the ashes. ⁹Then his wife said to him, "Are you still holding to your innocence? Curse God and die!" ¹⁰But he said to her, "You speak as foolish women do. We accept good things from God; should we not accept evil?" Through all this, Job did not sin in what he said.

Job's Three Friends. ¹¹Now when three of Job's friends heard of all the misfortune that had come upon him, they

and if he has seen his "servant Job" who remains "blameless and upright, fearing God and avoiding evil" (2:3). In still a further affirmation of Job, God accuses the Satan of manipulation in order to harm Job "without cause."

The Satan replies "skin for skin," a short saying that probably means, if you harm someone's skin, they will harm yours in turn. His principle of human behavior is that people may remain faithful when you take their things or their loved ones, but if you attack their bodies and threaten their lives, they will do anything. The Satan applies his principle to Job, insisting that Job will "curse you to your face" (2:5). Again without explanation, God relinquishes Job into the Satan's power. The only constraint on Satan is that he preserve Job's life.

2:7-10 Job's second test

Satan goes forth again and afflicts Job with severe boils that cover his body. To convey the horror of Job's physical condition, the narrator mentions the simple detail of a potsherd, a piece of broken pottery Job uses for wound-scraping as he sits on the ash heap (2:8). Job's nameless wife appears only in this scene, but her question intones a theme of both the prologue and the book. "Are you still holding to your innocence?," she asks. The Hebrew word translated "innocence" also means "integrity" or "wholeness" in the sense of deeply held honesty and blamelessness. Job's wife's motivations have provoked debate among interpreters. When she advises him to curse God and die, is she betraying him? In the ancient world, people believed cursing God brought certain death. Does his wife want him to die because she cannot bear to see him suffer? Or is her question a literary device to provoke Job's response? Everything comes from God, he proclaims, so should we not accept both good and evil? Job has passed the second test in patient fidelity.

2:11-13 The friends

Job's three friends hear of his tragedy and travel to see him, but they do not recognize him, so altered is he by his suffering. So stunned are they,

set out each one from his own place: Eliphaz from Teman, Bildad from Shuh, and Zophar from Naamath. They met and journeyed together to give him sympathy and comfort. [12]But when, at a distance, they lifted up their eyes and did not recognize him, they began to weep aloud; they tore their cloaks and threw dust into the air over their heads. [13]Then

they sat down upon the ground with him seven days and seven nights, but none of them spoke a word to him; for they saw how great was his suffering.

II. First Cycle of Speeches

3 **Job's Complaint.** [1]After this, Job opened his mouth and cursed his day. [2]Job spoke out and said:

---

they can find no words adequate to comfort him. They lament, tear their clothes, and put dust on their heads according to ancient mourning rituals. For a week they sit with him, mercifully silent, and perhaps numbed themselves, companions who see "how great was his suffering" (2:13). Their silent companionship may be their deepest act of friendship.

FIRST ROUND OF SPEECHES

Job 3:1–14:22

To cross from the prose prologue into the poetry in the book is to move into an altered world. Job is no longer the "patient man" of popular opinion but an enraged, impatient, and broken human. His friends, provoked by his outburst in chapter 3, also break their silence and offer advice to comfort and guide him into their version of the "truth"of his situation. Job's suffering expands in the poetic speeches for they add to his suffering internal anguish that compounds his pain. His friends fail to understand him and cannot relinquish their belief that he must be guilty of sin and so he must have caused his own suffering. Job himself has no other explanation for his overwhelming misery than that God has betrayed him. Together the speeches of Job and his friends offer conflicting interpretations of Job's suffering without indicating which one might be correct. This mode of theological debate encourages readers to weigh each view and to come to terms with the drama of Job's life themselves and perhaps also with the suffering within and around them.

3:1-10 Job curses his birth

Job curses both the day of his birth (3:1-6) and the night of his conception (3:7-10), two continuous moments in the creation of his life. His curse is actually a series of wishes, impossible appeals, not only to undo his life but also to unmake, to cancel out God's creation of his birthday. As a way to develop dramatic tension, the poem withholds the reason for his curse

15

Bronze sculpture of Job by Fr. Hugh Witzmann, O.S.B., Saint John's Abbey, Collegeville, Minnesota

³Perish the day on which I was
born,
the night when they said, "The
child is a boy!"
⁴May that day be darkness:
may God above not care for it,
may light not shine upon it!
⁵May darkness and gloom claim it,
clouds settle upon it,
blackness of day affright it!
⁶May obscurity seize that night;
may it not be counted among
the days of the year,
nor enter into the number of the
months!
⁷May that night be barren;
let no joyful outcry greet it!
⁸Let them curse it who curse the
Sea,
those skilled at disturbing
Leviathan!

⁹May the stars of its twilight be
darkened;
may it look for daylight, but
have none,
nor gaze on the eyes of the
dawn,
¹⁰Because it did not keep shut the
doors of the womb
to shield my eyes from trouble!
¹¹Why did I not die at birth,
come forth from the womb and
expire?
¹²Why did knees receive me,
or breasts nurse me?
¹³For then I should have lain down
and been tranquil;
had I slept, I should then have
been at rest
¹⁴With kings and counselors of the
earth
who rebuilt what were ruins

---

until verse ten. Prior to that, Job presents his suffering as part of the larger cosmic battle between light and darkness, order and chaos, life and death. Upon the day of his birth, he heaps a series of synonyms for darkness. He wishes to obliterate his day of birth from the calendar, as if it were possible to reach back in time and blot out his life from human history. Job wants to turn the day of his birth, normally a time of joy, into empty gloom. Daylight should turn to darkness, no light should shine, darkness should claim his day, and the dark night itself should frighten the day from even existing.

When Job steps back further in time to the night of his conception, he wishes to destroy the joyful night of his parents' love-making and the beginning of his life in the womb (3:7-10). Underlying his curse of the night are ancient Canaanite myths in which chaos struggles with order and life with death. Chaos was represented as the sea and sometimes as a mythic sea monster, here called "Leviathan" (3:8). Job desperately seeks a mysterious group of people who are able to raise up Leviathan to help him curse his conception. The poem poetically turns the night into a person who cannot find the morning light or gaze at the "eyes of the dawn" (3:9). The climax of the poem comes when Job finally proclaims the reason for his curses—the night did not shut the door to his mother's womb (3:10). Had he never been born or conceived, he would not have to face his present troubles.

¹⁵Or with princes who had gold
and filled their houses with
silver.
¹⁶Or why was I not buried away
like a stillborn child,
like babies that have never seen
the light?
¹⁷There the wicked cease from
troubling,
there the weary are at rest.
¹⁸The captives are at ease together,
and hear no overseer's voice.
¹⁹Small and great are there;
the servant is free from the
master.
²⁰Why is light given to the toilers,
life to the bitter in spirit?

²¹They wait for death and it does
not come;
they search for it more than for
hidden treasures.
²²They rejoice in it exultingly,
and are glad when they find the
grave:
²³A man whose path is hidden from
him,
one whom God has hemmed in!
²⁴For to me sighing comes more
readily than food;
my groans well forth like water.
²⁵For what I feared overtakes me;
what I dreaded comes upon me.
²⁶I have no peace nor ease;
I have no rest, for trouble has
come!

3:11-19 Job's despair

Job elaborates on his desire never to have been born with a series of questions about his birth (3:11-12). Since his conception was unavoidable, he would rather have been a stillborn or an abandoned infant with no one to nurse him. Then death would have come quickly, and he would be at rest rather than living in turmoil and pain. Death attracts him because it is a state of rest, free of pain. He imagines the world of the dead as a place occupied by many elite people who, in a democracy of the underworld, rest together with captives and slaves. In death everyone is free from oppression and from distinctions of class. Small and great are the same. To be there is better than to be alive in misery.

3:20-26 Why does anyone suffer?

Job's suffering expands his imagination and compassion. He moves in his mind from the world of the dead to the plight of other suffering people. His afflictions lead him to wonder why anyone suffers, why anyone would know so much anguish to make them long for death and to desire the grave. Job's sudden and colossal misery enables the once rich, powerful man to see beyond his own world to the larger torments of others. In Job's view, the reason people suffer is because God "hems" them in (3:23). Job sighs and groans and has discovered that he has little control over anything. Death is preferable because in death there is rest.

4 **Eliphaz's First Speech.** ¹Then Eliphaz the Temanite answered and said:

²If someone attempts a word with you, would you mind?
How can anyone refrain from speaking?
³Look, you have instructed many, and made firm their feeble hands.
⁴Your words have upheld the stumbler;
you have strengthened faltering knees.
⁵But now that it comes to you, you are impatient;
when it touches you, you are dismayed.

⁶Is not your piety a source of confidence,
and your integrity of life your hope?
⁷Reflect now, what innocent person perishes?
Where are the upright destroyed?
⁸As I see it, those who plow mischief and sow trouble will reap them.
⁹By the breath of God they perish, and by the blast of his wrath they are consumed.
¹⁰Though the lion roars, though the king of beasts cries out,
yet the teeth of the young lions are broken;

4:1–5:26 Eliphaz's first speech

Eliphaz from Teman is the most gentle of Job's three friends, all of whom are deeply rooted in the theology that people bring suffering upon themselves. Often called the "theology of retribution," the thinking is that if you do good things, you receive good things in return, and vice versa. Across the book, Job's friends will defend this view and interpret Job's life through it. But no matter their theology, the three friends care deeply for Job and wish to see him released from his suffering.

Respectfully, Eliphaz asks Job if he is willing to hear, if he is open to wise counsel. Implying that Job was once a vocal proponent of the theology of his friends, Eliphaz reminds him of his past support of people who faltered along life's journey (4:3-4). Now Job must preach to himself. With a rhetorical question, Eliphaz goes to the heart of the theology Job once shared with these friends (4:7). In his view, the innocent and the upright do not perish. Instead, they are safe and therefore Job can face the future in confidence.

Using a style of argument typical of wisdom literature, Eliphaz contrasts the fate of the innocent with the fate of trouble-makers (4:8-11). "Those who plow mischief" will get what they deserve, because God's angry breath will destroy them. The moral dynamic is clear; humans determine their own fate and Job must choose which group, the innocent or the wicked, he wishes to be among. And again using a common speech form of wisdom, Eliphaz speaks in proverb-like sayings that draw wisdom from the animal and plant

¹¹The old lion perishes for lack of
   prey,
   and the cubs of the lioness are
   scattered.
¹²A word was stealthily brought to
   me,
   my ear caught a whisper of it.
¹³In my thoughts during visions of
   the night,
   when deep sleep falls on
   mortals,
¹⁴Fear came upon me, and
   shuddering,
   that terrified me to the bone.
¹⁵Then a spirit passed before me,
   and the hair of my body stood
   on end.

¹⁶It paused, but its likeness I could
   not recognize;
   a figure was before my eyes,
   in silence I heard a voice:
¹⁷"Can anyone be more in the right
   than God?
   Can mortals be more blameless
   than their Maker?
¹⁸Look, he puts no trust in his
   servants,
   and even with his messengers
   he finds fault.
¹⁹How much more with those who
   dwell in houses of clay,
   whose foundation is in the dust,
   who are crushed more easily
   than a moth!

world. His reference to lions is not connected grammatically to the fate of the wicked, but it probably means that even these powerful beasts have to put up with travail and loss, so Job should expect no less.

Eliphaz claims that theological authority for his advice comes from his experience of "visions of the night," a dream-like revelation experienced by him alone (4:12-21). A spirit visits, frightens, and questions him, and then answers the questions. All creatures are sinful before God, even heavenly beings. Humans, made only of clay and dust, are even more sinful than corrupt denizens of the spirit world. Humans die and may never learn wisdom, presumably the wisdom of their true sinful condition. Depicting the fragility of human life, the visiting spirit speaks of human bodies as houses and tents, temporary dwellings that crush, shatter, or pluck up easily (4:19-21). That life is fragile and humans sinful should be a warning to Job.

Eliphaz's advice grows less gentle when he points to Job's isolation in his suffering (5:1-2). There are no holy ones to whom Job might appeal for help. Whereas some interpreters believe Eliphaz's claim about holy ones is a putdown of ancient beliefs in lesser gods who intervene with the high god, others think Eliphaz is merely underscoring the vast gap between humans and the spirit world. Job cannot expect assistance; all rests with him alone. Although Eliphaz does not say Job is an impatient fool directly, in typical wisdom style, he implies as much. The fool's fate includes loss of his household and the endangerment of children (5:4). In his most callous and insensitive statement, Eliphaz interprets the tragic death of Job's children as both something avoidable and the result of Job's own malfeasance (5:7).

²⁰Morning or evening they may be
  shattered;
    unnoticed, they perish forever.
²¹The pegs of their tent are plucked
  up;
    they die without knowing
      wisdom."

5 ¹Call now! Will anyone respond to
  you?
    To which of the holy ones will
      you turn?
²Surely impatience kills the fool
  and indignation slays the
    simpleton.
³I have seen a fool spreading his
  roots,
    but I cursed his household
      suddenly:
⁴May his children be far from safety;

may they be crushed at the gate
  without a rescuer.
⁵What they have reaped may the
  hungry eat up,
    or God take away by blight,
      or the thirsty swallow their
        substance.
⁶For not from dust does mischief
  come,
    nor from the soil does trouble
      sprout.
⁷Human beings beget mischief
  as sparks fly upward.
⁸In your place, I would appeal to
  God,
    and to God I would state my
      plea.
⁹He does things great and
  unsearchable,

Pain and loss are clear and understandable for Eliphaz. He says this in a number of striking ways (5:2-7). The fool's impatience slays him; the fool spreads his roots but around him his family collapses; the hungry will eat what they reap, and mischief does not emerge from the ground. In other words, suffering is not built into the created order of the world; instead, humans manufacture it. Accordingly, Job has brought his anguish upon himself. Eliphaz's belief that humans are responsible for what happens in life, his "theology of retribution," also contains hope for Job. If he caused his pain, he can also act to remove it.

Eliphaz truly wants his friend to escape his suffering and live a renewed life (5:8-16). His advice rests on his assumptions about Job's situation. If I were you, "I would appeal to God, and to God I would state my plea" (5:8). Job did not do so in his cursing laments in chapter three. Parallel statements about God's treatment of the earth and its inhabitants emphasize the urgency of Eliphaz's hopes for his friend (5:10-13). To motivate Job to appeal to God, Eliphaz points to saving characteristics of the divine. God is creator and rain giver, rescuer of the lowly and mournful, and frustrator of the schemes and craftiness of the so-called "wise." It is the poor whom God saves, so "the needy have hope" (5:16). Eliphaz reminds Job of a theological tradition of which Job has long been a part; God is on the side of the broken and the humble.

*Job's friends, Eliphaz, Bildad, and Zophar, come to give Job sympathy
and comfort (Job 2:1-3).*

things marvelous and innumerable.

¹⁰He gives rain upon the earth
and sends water upon the fields;

¹¹He sets up the lowly on high,
and those who mourn are raised
to safety.

¹²He frustrates the plans of the
cunning,
so that their hands achieve no
success;

¹³He catches the wise in their own
ruses,
and the designs of the crafty are
routed.

¹⁴They meet with darkness in the
daytime,
at noonday they grope as
though it were night.

¹⁵But he saves the poor from the
sword of their mouth,
from the hand of the mighty.

¹⁶Thus the needy have hope,
and iniquity closes its mouth.

¹⁷Happy the one whom God
reproves!
The Almighty's discipline do
not reject.

¹⁸For he wounds, but he binds up;
he strikes, but his hands give
healing.

¹⁹Out of six troubles he will deliver
you,
and at the seventh no evil shall
touch you.

²⁰In famine he will deliver you from
death,
and in war from the power of
the sword;

²¹From the scourge of the tongue
you shall be hidden,
and you shall not fear approaching ruin.

²²At ruin and want you shall laugh;
the beasts of the earth, do not
fear.

²³With the stones of the field shall
your covenant be,

Eliphaz then moves from the subject of how God behaves to a theological interpretation of Job's predicament (5:16-27). Using the "happy is the one" saying common among wisdom sayings (e.g., Ps 1:1 and Prov 29:18), Eliphaz thinks God's reprimand is a blessing that should not be rejected. He assumes that Job's suffering is a punishment to benefit him. Job will escape his suffering because of God's character. God both wounds and binds up, smites and heals (5:18). Eliphaz applies his thinking directly to Job's life by changing from third person plural speech (they) about the unfortunate in general to the second person singular "you" of direct address. God will deliver "you" from evils, threats, swords, wars, scandals, fear, want, and beasts of the earth (5:18-23).

Extremely appealing blessings cap Eliphaz's advice to Job (5:23-27). He continues to address Job directly to assure him he will be in covenant with the earth and its inhabitants (5:23). Job will be at peace with stones and beasts alike. He will live in security in a household lacking nothing; he will see his offspring and live to old age, like grain in its season (5:26). Eliphaz concludes with a clinching warrant for the advice he has offered Job. "We," presumably, he and his wise friends, have "searched" it out (5:27). From

and the wild beasts shall be at
    peace with you.
²⁴And you shall know that your
    tent is secure;
  taking stock of your household,
    you shall miss nothing.
²⁵You shall know that your descen-
    dants are many,
  and your offspring like the grass
    of the earth.
²⁶You shall approach the grave in
    full vigor,
  as a shock of grain comes in at
    its season.
²⁷See, this we have searched out; so
    it is!
  This we have heard, and you
    should know.

6 **Job's First Reply.** ¹Then Job answered
and said:

²Ah, could my anguish but be mea-
    sured
  and my calamity laid with it in
    the scales,
³They would now outweigh the
    sands of the sea!
  Because of this I speak without
    restraint.
⁴For the arrows of the Almighty are
    in me,

and my spirit drinks in their
    poison;
  the terrors of God are arrayed
    against me.
⁵Does the wild donkey bray when it
    has grass?
  Does the ox low over its fodder?
⁶Can anything insipid be eaten
    without salt?
  Is there flavor in the white of an
    egg?
⁷I refuse to touch them;
  they are like loathsome food to
    me.
⁸Oh, that I might have my request,
  and that God would grant what
    I long for:
⁹Even that God would decide to
    crush me,
  that he would put forth his hand
    and cut me off!
¹⁰Then I should still have consolation
  and could exult through
    unremitting pain,
  because I have not transgressed
    the commands of the
    Holy One.
¹¹What strength have I that I should
    endure,
  and what is my limit that I
    should be patient?

---

the sages' long study of human experience, they have known that Eliphaz
speaks the truth, or so he claims.

6:1–7:21 Job's reply to Eliphaz

Set next to Eliphaz's tranquil vision of Job's future, Job's response appears all the more bitter. His experience no longer complies with Eliphaz's
optimistic picture of the life of the faithful. Whereas Eliphaz believes Job
must be responsible for his suffering, so he can also anticipate a beautiful future once he appeals to God, Job believes God has viciously turned
against him. Nor does Job believe Eliphaz has heard or understood him.
His suffering is so enormous that it cannot be measured, for it is heavier
than "the sands of the sea" (6:2-3).

¹²Have I the strength of stones,
 or is my flesh of bronze?
¹³Have I no helper,
 and has my good sense deserted
  me?
¹⁴A friend owes kindness to one in
 despair,
 though he has forsaken the fear
  of the Almighty.
¹⁵My companions are undepend-
 able as a wadi,
 as watercourses that run dry in
  the wadies;
¹⁶Though they may be black with
 ice,
 and with snow heaped upon
  them,
¹⁷Yet once they flow, they cease to
 be;
 in the heat, they disappear from
  their place.
¹⁸Caravans wander from their
 routes;
 they go into the wasteland and
  perish.

¹⁹The caravans of Tema search,
 the companies of Sheba have
  hopes;
²⁰They are disappointed, though
 they were confident;
 they come there and are frustrated.
²¹It is thus that you have now become for me;
 you see a terrifying thing and
  are afraid.
²²Have I said, "Give me something,
 make a bribe on my behalf from
  your possessions"?
²³Or "Deliver me from the hand of
 the enemy,
 redeem me from oppressors"?
²⁴Teach me, and I will be silent;
 make me understand how I
  have erred.
²⁵How painful honest words can be;
 yet how unconvincing is your
  argument!
²⁶Do you consider your words as
 proof,

Job's complaint about the enormity of his misery indicates the depth of the chaos in which he now lives (6:2-7). His immeasurable pain leads him to speak freely. Without restraint, he interprets his suffering as the consequence of God's attack on him. Like a vicious hunter, God shoots poison-tipped arrows into him (6:4). God is a terrorist who both attacks and poisons him. Like his friends, Job also uses proverb-like sayings from the animal world to give authority to his speech. Neither the wild donkey nor the ox make noise without reason, and so Job, too, has reasons for his emotional lament.

Verses six and seven are obscure even in the Hebrew, but they focus on food as a metaphor for life. Job's food is tasteless and loathsome to him.

After his sharp outburst in the previous verses, it is as if he were so alienated from God, he cannot even pray (6:8-10). Job does not address God but speaks indirectly in a wishful manner about the deity. He wants God to respond to a startling request—that God would crush him and cut him off. His death would be a comfort because he is innocent. He insists he has been obedient to divine commands and, therefore, did not create his own suffering, as Eliphaz maintains. The rhetorical questions of the next three

but the sayings of a desperate
  man as wind?
²⁷You would even cast lots for the
  orphan,
  and would barter over your
  friend!
²⁸Come, now, give me your attention;
  surely I will not lie to your face.
²⁹Think it over; let there be no injustice.
  Think it over; I still am right.
³⁰Is there insincerity on my tongue,
  or cannot my taste discern falsehood?

7 ¹Is not life on earth a drudgery,
  its days like those of a hireling?

²Like a slave who longs for the
  shade,
  a hireling who waits for wages,
³So I have been assigned months of
  futility,
  and troubled nights have been
  counted off for me.
⁴When I lie down I say, "When shall
  I arise?"
  then the night drags on;
  I am filled with restlessness
  until the dawn.
⁵My flesh is clothed with worms
  and scabs;
  my skin cracks and festers;
⁶My days are swifter than a weaver's
  shuttle;

verses reinforce Job's despair and desire to endure no longer (6:11-14). He ponders his own strength, his limits, and his support group, and all fall short.

Particularly unsatisfactory is the support of his friends (6:14-17). Job's remarks about his friends increase readers' sense of his isolation. Rather than speaking directly to his friends, he speaks about them in the third person as though they are not present. The ideal friend owes kindness to one "in despair," even if he has abandoned the "fear of the Almighty" (6:14). "Fear of God" in the Old Testament means a spirit of true religion, of obedience and awe before God. Hence, friends owe loyalty to the wounded. Even if he has broken loyalty with God, they should not. In Job's culture, loyalty among friends is of very high value. Job's friends fail him like a dried up stream in the desert or a raging, icy torrent in winter (6:15-16). Jeremiah makes similar accusations against God who, like a treacherous stream, disappears in times of need (Jer 15:17).

Though the next verses appear to change the imagery from water courses to caravans, they are probably continuing the same search for reliable sources of water (6:18-21). Merchant caravans may leave their routes to find water in desert streams only to be frustrated, as Job is with his friends who offer him no nourishment. That only one friend has spoken so far in the book may not be important for Job's conclusion, if he understands Eliphaz to be speaking for all of them. But Job's language of the deceptive waters and the frustrated caravans are not offered indirectly as in Eliphaz's style of speech. Job uses second person address to apply the deception to his friends. "It is thus you have now become for me" (6:21). Then Job interprets

they come to an end without
hope.
[7]Remember that my life is like the
wind;
my eye will not see happiness
again.
[8]The eye that now sees me shall no
more behold me;
when your eye is on me, I shall
be gone.
[9]As a cloud dissolves and vanishes,

so whoever goes down to Sheol
shall not come up.
[10]They shall not return home again;
their place shall know them no
more.
[11]My own utterance I will not
restrain;
I will speak in the anguish of
my spirit;
I will complain in the bitterness
of my soul.

the cause of their betrayal. They see and "are afraid." They see Job's terrible suffering that might become their fate, too, if their theology proves wrong. Fear blinds them to his true circumstances.

The subject of their friendship continues to occupy Job's thoughts for the rest of the chapter (6:22-30). He wants to know how he has failed them, or if he has asked too much from them. Humbly he begs them to teach him where he has gone wrong. Once he knows, he will stop speaking. But he does not believe he is wrong for he accuses them of dishonest speech. He mocks their words as lacking proof and having the windy quality of the desperate. He attacks their moral character as callous enough to "cast lots" for an orphan and to sell away a friend. Then he pleads with them for a full and attentive hearing and tries to convince them of his honesty and his innocence (6:30).

Job now reflects on human misery in general and his experience of it in particular (7:1-10). Rhetorical questions embrace the lot of humanity. Is human life not drudgery, the life of a "hireling," a laborer with little or nothing in the way of rights or pay or dignity? Like a slave without protection, Job too lives in misery. The verb translated, "I have been assigned" indicates Job's self-understanding as a victim of some design (7:3). He laments his nights when he talks to himself, is restless, and his skin crawls (cf. 2:7-8). His days, in contrast to his nights, are brief and hopeless (7:10). Despair prevails in his imagination, for he cannot conceive of any future different from the present except for death, an event he expounds with images of life's fleetingness. Eyes will no longer see him, clouds will dissolve like those who go to the underworld, and the dead will not return home.

But it is Job's very despair that empowers him to speak and to express his resistance to God's designs upon him. He has nothing to lose, so he will not even try to be quiet (7:11). He hurls a bold challenge to God. Does God

¹²Am I the Sea, or the dragon,
   that you place a watch over me?
¹³When I say, "My bed shall comfort
   me,
   my couch shall ease my com-
      plaint,"
¹⁴Then you frighten me with
      dreams
   and terrify me with visions,
¹⁵So that I should prefer
      strangulation
   and death rather than my
      existence.
¹⁶I waste away: I will not live
      forever;
   let me alone, for my days are
      but a breath.
¹⁷What are human beings, that you
      make much of them,
   or pay them any heed?

¹⁸You observe them every morning
   and try them at every moment!
¹⁹How long before you look away
      from me,
   and let me alone till I swallow
      my spit?
²⁰If I sin, what do I do to you,
   O watcher of mortals?
Why have you made me your
      target?
Why should I be a burden for
      you?
²¹Why do you not pardon my
      offense,
   or take away my guilt?
For soon I shall lie down in the
      dust;
   and should you seek me I shall
      be gone.

---

think he is a sea monster or the sea itself, those mythic images of unbridled force and chaos that Job mentioned in 3:8? Job accuses God of watching him and attacking him as if he were one of the sea creatures, and he demands to know why God makes him a target. In Job's view, God assaults him without reason and misunderstands his own being. He cannot escape this treachery in the comfort and oblivion of sleep because God continues to attack him even in his dreams. He would prefer to die and, unlike most religious people, asks only for God to leave him alone (7:16).

To express his plight, Job alludes to Psalm 8 and inverts its meaning. The question of the psalm, "What are human beings that you make so much of them, mortals that you care for them?" (Ps 8:5, NRSV) becomes in Job's mouth not thanksgiving for God's care but a promise of judgment, threat, and menacing presence. Job's despair continues to drive him. Depending on how one translates verse 20—Job either acknowledges he is a sinner, "If I sin" (NABRE) or in other translations, "Though I sinned"—the consequences are the same. God does not pardon guilt of anyone. But even if Job has sinned, he has done nothing to deserve the calamities that have befallen him. He calls God a "watcher" of humans (7:20), not to speak of divine protection but to accuse God of vigilance in search of human sin. Like a petulant child, he reminds God of his mortality. Time is running out and the two of them are split asunder.

8 Bildad's First Speech. ¹Bildad the Shuhite answered and said:

²How long will you utter such things?
The words from your mouth are a mighty wind!
³Does God pervert judgment,
does the Almighty pervert justice?
⁴If your children have sinned against him
and he has left them in the grip of their guilt,
⁵Still, if you yourself have recourse to God
and make supplication to the Almighty,
⁶Should you be blameless and upright,
surely now he will rouse himself for you
and restore your rightful home.
⁷Though your beginning was small,
your future will flourish indeed.
⁸Inquire of the former generations,
pay attention to the experience of their ancestors—
⁹As we are but of yesterday and have no knowledge,
because our days on earth are but a shadow—
¹⁰Will they not teach you and tell you
and utter their words of understanding?
¹¹Can the papyrus grow up without mire?
Can the reed grass flourish without water?

8:1-22 Bildad's first speech

When Job's second friend speaks, it is to jump to God's defense and to call Job a chattering windbag. God's justice cannot be challenged, argues Bildad. After he applauds God's reliable governance of the world, he strikes a piercing blow against his friend. Indirectly but unmistakably, he interprets the death of Job's children as the result of their sin (8:4). Bildad cannot think for a minute that the innocent would perish. Like Eliphaz, Bildad believes there is still hope for Job (8:5-7). If he appeals to God and is "blameless and upright," God will act on his behalf. Readers, of course, know from the prologue that Job is "blameless and upright" (1:1). But for Bildad, Job's moral state has become a matter of doubt. Even so, if Job appeals to God in righteousness, then God will restore him as if nothing ever happened.

Besides turning back to God, Bildad advises Job to appeal to the ancestors and the wise traditions of the past that have sustained many (8:8-19). What they will teach Job is the dismal fate of the wicked, once again implying that Job is among them and must take action to escape their company. Bildad offers a proverb drawn from the natural world to make his point (8:11-13). Papyrus and reeds grow only in water; even so humans live only in God. God-forgetters will perish like the "gossamer" threads of a spider's web (8:14). The godless appear to be filled with life energy, but they cannot grow among the rocks, and they have no safe place.

¹²While it is yet green and uncut,
    it withers quicker than any
        grass.
¹³So is the end of everyone who
        forgets God,
    and so shall the hope of the
        godless perish.
¹⁴His confidence is but a gossamer
        thread,
    his trust is a spider's house.
¹⁵He shall lean upon his house, but
        it shall not stand;
    he shall cling to it, but it shall
        not endure.
¹⁶He thrives in full sun,
    and over his garden his shoots
        go forth;
¹⁷About a heap of stones his roots
        are entwined;
    among the rocks he takes hold.
¹⁸Yet if one tears him from his place,
    it will disown him: "I have
        never seen you!"
¹⁹There he lies rotting beside the
        road,
    and out of the soil another
        sprouts.
²⁰Behold, God will not cast away
        the upright;
    neither will he take the hand of
        the wicked.

²¹Once more will he fill your mouth
        with laughter
    and your lips with rejoicing.
²²Those who hate you shall be
        clothed with shame,
    and the tent of the wicked shall
        be no more.

9 Job's Second Reply. ¹Then Job
answered and said:

²I know well that it is so;
    but how can anyone be in the
        right before God?
³Should one wish to contend with
        him,
    he could not answer him once in
        a thousand times.
⁴God is wise in heart and mighty in
        strength;
    who has withstood him and
        remained whole?
⁵He removes the mountains before
        they know it;
    he overturns them in his anger.
⁶He shakes the earth out of its
        place,
    and the pillars beneath it
        tremble.
⁷He commands the sun, and it does
        not rise;
    he seals up the stars.

In these allusions, Bildad places Job among the godless but, confident that God overcomes the suffering of the righteous, he also promises Job a glowing future. Job will again know overflowing laughter and his lips will rejoice even as his enemies meet their demise (8:21-22).

9:1–10:22 Job's reply to Bildad

In anguish, Job affirms what Bildad had just said, "I know well that it is so" (9:1). Certain that no human can stand before God in complete innocence, he knows the human condition is sinful and broken. Once he had been a proponent of his friend's theology, but now his experience challenges his old theology. Yet no new understanding of suffering and God's relationship has emerged to ease his way. He is in a liminal position outside of solid explanations.

⁸He alone stretches out the heavens
   and treads upon the back of the
   sea.
⁹He made the Bear and Orion,
   the Pleiades and the constellations of the south;
¹⁰He does things great and unsearchable,
   things marvelous and innumerable.
¹¹Should he come near me, I do not
   see him;
   should he pass by, I am not
   aware of him;
¹²Should he seize me forcibly, who
   can resist?

Who can say to him, "What are
   you doing?"
¹³He is God and he does not relent;
   the helpers of Rahab bow
   beneath him.
¹⁴How then could I give him any
   answer,
   or choose out arguments against
   him!
¹⁵Even though I were right, I could
   not answer,
   but should rather beg for what
   was due me.
¹⁶If I appealed to him and he
   answered me,
   I could not believe that he
   would listen to me;

By contrast to human creatureliness, God's awesomeness intimidates Job (9:3-13). The Hebrew word translated "to contend with" has legal implications (9:3). If Job wanted to take God to court, he would be unable to speak because God's power and distance from humans contribute to Job's feelings of helplessness. Job extols God's strength in a hymn containing a series of parallel verbs about divine deeds (9:4-11). But unlike other creation hymns that sing of the harmonious beauty of God's creative work (Gen 1; Ps 104), in Job's hymn, God's deeds are terrifying. God removes and overturns mountains, shakes the earth out of its place, seals off sun and stars.

This God is dangerous, beyond comprehension, and invisible even when present (9:11-21). Divine presence is not a blessing for Job. God might seize him and who would be strong enough to resist? Even the helpers of the powerful, mythic sea monster, here called "Rahab" (9:13; cf. 3:8) cannot resist the relentless power of God. If God overpowers them, all the more, God's presence silences Job (9:14). Even if Job were to get God to come to court, Job's fear would force him to say the opposite of what he intended. God would not hear him out and would surely overcome him with a storm (some translations read "tempest"), a great whirlwind (see 38:1). Even if Job is in the right, he has no hope in a courtroom. He declares he is innocent, but he cannot experience the legal results of innocence, so he despairs (9:21).

Job's suffering leads him to reflect more broadly on the inadequacies of divine justice in the world (9:22-24). God treats the good and the bad equally, destroying both at whim. God gives the earth into the power of the wicked and even blinds judges to the plight of the innocent. If the powerful

¹⁷With a storm he might overwhelm
me,
and multiply my wounds for
nothing;
¹⁸He would not allow me to draw
breath,
but might fill me with bitter
griefs.
¹⁹If it be a question of strength, he is
mighty;
or of judgment, who will call
him to account?
²⁰Though I were right, my own
mouth might condemn me;
were I innocent, it might put me
in the wrong.
²¹I am innocent, but I cannot know it;
I despise my life.

²²It is all one! therefore I say:
Both the innocent and the
wicked he destroys.
²³When the scourge slays suddenly,
he scoffs at the despair of the
innocent.
²⁴The earth is given into the hands
of the wicked;
he covers the faces of its judges.
If it is not he, who then is it?
²⁵My days are swifter than a runner,
they flee away; they see no
happiness;
²⁶They shoot by like skiffs of reed,
like an eagle swooping upon its
prey.
²⁷If I say: I will forget my
complaining,

God is not the one who overturns justice in the world, then who is it? Job asks. He turns again to the fragility of his life, speaking in the first person to describe his pains and loss, but he knows God will not recognize his innocence (9:25-31). There is nothing he can do to establish it. Using second person speech, he accuses God of altering the facts, for God has plunged him into the ditch (9:31). Physical cleaning would symbolize his innocence. In Job's imagination that cannot be accomplished.

A court of law is one place wherein he might declare his innocence, but God is not human, and the gap between them is so enormous, only an arbiter or mediator could help Job. He imagines someone who could control God and protect him from God's might. Such a mediator could make a meeting between them possible and Job might then speak without fear. But this hope is contrary to fact, for no one can tell God what to do. Job sinks back into despair and hates his life (10:1a).

Rather than being cowed by his fearful despair, Job speaks for another chapter and grows more courageous. He announces his determination to speak the truth before God, imagining what he will say and demanding justice (10:1b-2). Boldly, he demands an accounting of God's treatment of him (10:3-7). His questions challenge God's very identity as a divine being. He accuses God of acting no differently than a human oppressor who delights in the pain of others. He reminds God of their deep relationship, for Job is the work of God's hands (10:3). God knows Job is innocent yet searches for sin and guilt in him regardless of the true state of Job's heart.

I will lay aside my sadness and
    be of good cheer,
²⁸Then I am in dread of all my
    pains;
I know that you will not hold
    me innocent.
²⁹It is I who will be accounted
    guilty;
why then should I strive in
    vain?
³⁰If I should wash myself with soap
    and cleanse my hands with lye,
³¹Yet you would plunge me in the
    ditch,
so that my garments would
    abhor me.
³²For he is not a man like myself,
    that I should answer him,
that we should come together in
    judgment.
³³Would that there were an arbiter
    between us,
who could lay his hand upon us
    both
³⁴and withdraw his rod from
    me,
So that his terrors did not frighten
    me;
³⁵that I might speak without
    being afraid of him.
Since this is not the case with me,
    ¹⁰:¹I loathe my life.

10 I will give myself up to complaint;
I will speak from the bitterness
    of my soul.
²I will say to God: Do not put me in
    the wrong!
Let me know why you oppose
    me.
³Is it a pleasure for you to oppress,
    to spurn the work of your
    hands,
and shine on the plan of the
    wicked?
⁴Have you eyes of flesh?
    Do you see as mortals see?
⁵Are your days like the days of a
    mortal,
and are your years like a human
    lifetime,
⁶That you seek for guilt in me
    and search after my sins,
⁷Even though you know that I am
    not wicked,
and that none can deliver me
    out of your hand?
⁸Your hands have formed me and
    fashioned me;
will you then turn and destroy
    me?
⁹Oh, remember that you fashioned
    me from clay!
Will you then bring me down to
    dust again?

Job switches rhetorical tactics from blaming interrogation to gracious appeal, returning to the intimate relationship God has had with him from the time of his conception (10:8-13). Unlike his curse of his conception and birth in chapter 3, this appeal emphasizes God's tender care in fashioning his being, knitting him together in his mother's womb (see Ps 139:13). God has forgotten this past relationship between them (10:13). The rest of the speech resumes Job's bitter attack on God (10:14-22). There is no hope for a just hearing for God watches, will not forgive, attacks, and hunts Job like a lion no matter whether he is guilty or innocent. Now Job resumes thinking about his birth as a tragedy God should have averted by not letting him be born. Now Job wants God to leave him alone as he faces death.

¹⁰Did you not pour me out like
   milk,
   and thicken me like cheese?
¹¹With skin and flesh you clothed
   me,
   with bones and sinews knit me
      together.
¹²Life and love you granted me,
   and your providence has
      preserved my spirit.
¹³Yet these things you have hidden
      in your heart;
   I know they are your purpose:
¹⁴If I should sin, you would keep a
      watch on me,
   and from my guilt you would
      not absolve me.
¹⁵If I should be wicked, alas for me!
   even if righteous, I dare not
      hold up my head,
   sated with shame, drenched in
      affliction!
¹⁶Should it lift up, you hunt me like
      a lion:
   repeatedly you show your
      wondrous power against
      me,
¹⁷You renew your attack upon me
   and multiply your harassment
      of me;
   in waves your troops come
      against me.
¹⁸Why then did you bring me forth
      from the womb?
   I should have died and no eye
      have seen me.
¹⁹I should be as though I had never
      lived;

I should have been taken from
   the womb to the grave.
²⁰Are not my days few? Stop!
   Let me alone, that I may recover
      a little
²¹Before I go whence I shall not re-
      turn,
   to the land of darkness and of
      gloom,
²²The dark, disordered land
   where darkness is the only light.

11 **Zophar's First Speech.** ¹And
   Zophar the Naamathite answered
and said:

²Should not many words be
      answered,
   or must the garrulous man nec-
      essarily be right?
³Shall your babblings keep others
      silent,
   and shall you deride and no one
      give rebuke?
⁴Shall you say: "My teaching is pure,
   and I am clean in your sight"?
⁵But oh, that God would speak,
   and open his lips against you,
⁶And tell you the secrets of wisdom,
   for good sense has two sides;
So you might learn that God
   overlooks some of your
      sinfulness.
⁷Can you find out the depths of
      God?
   or find out the perfection of the
      Almighty?
⁸It is higher than the heavens; what
      can you do?

11:1-20 Zophar's first speech

Job's third friend is immensely impatient with him. He thinks Job is
full of hot air, babbling words, and arrogant self-righteousness (11:2-3).
Job, he contends, has claimed doctrinal and ethical purity for himself. But
Zophar is confident that if God were to speak, Job would learn wisdom
and pay for his guilt. Zophar bases his authority on traditional theological

It is deeper than Sheol; what can
you know?
⁹It is longer than the earth in
measure,
and broader than the sea.
¹⁰If he should seize and imprison
or call to judgment, who then
could turn him back?
¹¹For he knows the worthless
and sees iniquity; will he then
ignore it?
¹²An empty head will gain
understanding,
when a colt of a wild jackass is
born human.
¹³If you set your heart aright
and stretch out your hands
toward him,
¹⁴If iniquity is in your hand, remove
it,
and do not let injustice dwell in
your tent,
¹⁵Surely then you may lift up your
face in innocence;
you may stand firm and
unafraid.
¹⁶For then you shall forget your
misery,
like water that has ebbed away
you shall regard it.
¹⁷Then your life shall be brighter
than the noonday;

its gloom shall become like the
morning,
¹⁸And you shall be secure, because
there is hope;
you shall look round you and lie
down in safety;
¹⁹you shall lie down and no one
will disturb you.
Many shall entreat your favor,
²⁰but the wicked, looking on,
shall be consumed with
envy.
Escape shall be cut off from them,
their only hope their last breath.

12 Job's Third Reply. ¹Then Job answered and said:

²No doubt you are the people
with whom wisdom shall die!
³But I have intelligence as well as
you;
I do not fall short of you;
for who does not know such
things as these?
⁴I have become the sport of my
neighbors:
"The one whom God answers
when he calls upon him,
The just, the perfect man," is a
laughingstock;
⁵The undisturbed esteem my down-
fall a disgrace

---

doctrine, expressed in a hymn praising divine power and knowledge (11:8-12). Humans cannot know the designs of God for they are impenetrable to humans. But then Zophar contradicts himself. He himself knows the mind of God regarding "worthless" people, a point he emphasizes with a proverb-like saying that indirectly attacks Job as an empty, untamable wild jackass (11:12).

Despite his scathing denunciation of Job, Zophar joins Eliphaz and Bildad to advise Job about how to escape from his suffering (11:13-19). The conditions he sets assume Job's guilt. Job must set his heart aright, abandon iniquity, and cast out injustice. Then he will have a future without fear or shame, and his misery will fade from memory like receding waters. The

such as awaits unsteady feet;
⁶Yet the tents of robbers are prosperous,
and those who provoke God are secure,
whom God has in his power.
⁷But now ask the beasts to teach you,
the birds of the air to tell you;
⁸Or speak to the earth to instruct you,
and the fish of the sea to inform you.
⁹Which of all these does not know
that the hand of God has done this?
¹⁰In his hand is the soul of every living thing,
and the life breath of all mortal flesh.
¹¹Does not the ear judge words
as the mouth tastes food?
¹²So with old age is wisdom,
and with length of days understanding.
¹³With him are wisdom and might;
his are counsel and understanding.
¹⁴If he knocks a thing down, there is no rebuilding;
if he imprisons, there is no release.

¹⁵He holds back the waters and there is drought;
he sends them forth and they overwhelm the land.
¹⁶With him are strength and prudence;
the misled and the misleaders are his.
¹⁷He sends counselors away barefoot,
makes fools of judges.
¹⁸He loosens the belt of kings,
ties a waistcloth on their loins.
¹⁹He sends priests away barefoot,
leads the powerful astray.
²⁰He silences the trusted adviser,
takes discretion from the elders.
²¹He pours shame on nobles,
the waistband of the strong he loosens.
²²He uncovers deep things from the darkness,
brings the gloom into the light.
²³He makes nations great and destroys them,
spreads peoples abroad and abandons them.
²⁴He takes understanding from the leaders of the land,
makes them wander in a pathless desert.

---

picture is utopian, for Job's life will be brighter than the noonday; he will live in safety and be at rest.

12:1–14:22 Job's reply to Zophar

Job counters Zophar's speech with denunciations of his own. Sarcastically, he ridicules his friends' advice as the product of wisdom they alone seem to possess. But immediately Job asserts his equal intelligence and skill in expressing wisdom (12:2-3). From the perspective of relationships of honor and shame typical of ancient Israelite culture, he describes his suffering from yet another angle (12:4-6). His neighbors' mockery disgraces him and amplifies his suffering, for he has lost his place in society. He names robbers and God-provokers among the prosperous in order to contradict

²⁵They grope in the darkness without light;
he makes them wander like drunkards.

13 ¹All this my eye has seen;
my ear has heard and perceived it.
²What you know, I also know;
I do not fall short of you.
³But I would speak with the Almighty;
I want to argue with God.
⁴But you gloss over falsehoods,
you are worthless physicians,
every one of you!
⁵Oh, that you would be altogether silent;
that for you would be wisdom!
⁶Hear now my argument
and listen to the accusations from my lips.
⁷Is it for God that you speak falsehood?
Is it for him that you utter deceit?

⁸Is it for him that you show partiality?
Do you make accusations on behalf of God?
⁹Will it be well when he shall search you out?
Can you deceive him as you do a mere human being?
¹⁰He will openly rebuke you
if in secret you show partiality.
¹¹Surely his majesty will frighten you
and dread of him fall upon you.
¹²Your reminders are ashy maxims,
your fabrications mounds of clay.
¹³Be silent! Let me alone that I may speak,
no matter what happens to me.
¹⁴I will carry my flesh between my teeth,
and take my life in my hand.
¹⁵Slay me though he might, I will wait for him;
I will defend my conduct before him.

---

his friends' theology. When he claims that humans can learn from living creatures, he turns his friends' wisdom tactics back on them because he draws opposite conclusions (12:7-10). Instead of claiming that other creatures teach God's providential care of the work, the beasts, birds, reptiles, and fish know God controls all that lives and human suffering.

In another hymn, Job reflects on God's strength (12:13-25). He portrays divine actions in the world, beginning mildly enough (12:13), but the examples of divine power he draws upon are violently fearsome. God breaks down, imprisons, creates drought, releases prisoners, imprisons kings, and disperses rather than gathers water. God overturns expectations concerning leaders, nations, and the patterns of just political relationships in the world. Though Job affirms traditional notions of divine power, he believes God's power is both unconstrained and destructive of human life.

From experience and observation as a sage, Job claims equality with his friends in discerning God's ways (13:1-2). Yet despite his belief that God is unpredictable and dangerous, he declares his desire to argue his case with God. His friends lie and he begs them to show their wisdom by being

¹⁶This shall be my salvation:
   no impious man can come into
     his presence.
¹⁷Pay close attention to my speech,
   give my statement a hearing.
¹⁸Behold, I have prepared my case,
   I know that I am in the right.
¹⁹If anyone can make a case against
   me,
   then I shall be silent and expire.
²⁰Two things only do not use
   against me,
   then from your presence I need
     not hide:
²¹Withdraw your hand far from me,
   do not let the terror of you
     frighten me.
²²Then call me, and I will respond;
   or let me speak first, and answer
     me.
²³What are my faults and my sins?

My misdeed, my sin make
   known to me!
²⁴Why do you hide your face
   and consider me your enemy?
²⁵Will you harass a wind-driven leaf
   or pursue a withered straw?
²⁶For you draw up bitter indict-
   ments against me,
   and punish in me the faults of
     my youth.
²⁷You put my feet in the stocks;
   you watch all my paths
   and trace out all my footsteps,
²⁸Though I wear out like a leather
   bottle,
   like a garment the moth has
     consumed.

14 ¹Man born of woman
   is short-lived and full of trouble,
²Like a flower that springs up and
   fades,

---

silent; God will rebuke them when judgment comes (13:4-13). His passion for speaking grows and he refuses to be silenced; he says he will go so far as to "carry my flesh between my teeth" (13:14). Although this expression does not occur elsewhere in the Old Testament, the next verse clarifies its meaning. Job will speak at the risk of his life. He will defend himself before God, even if God kills him. To speak before God would vindicate him, for no "impious" person can come before God (13:16). Job has prepared his case and reasserts his innocence but would be silent if anyone can build a case against him. Job's confidence rests in his belief that he has not committed any actions against God or humans that warrant his present suffering.

Job shifts from addressing his friends to speaking directly to God, a shift marked by a move from plural to singular verbs (13:20-27). Legal dealings inform Job's imagination about his relationship with God and provide a way for him to describe himself as one unjustly accused, imprisoned, and monitored. But the courtroom can also become a place in Job's hopes that will reveal his innocence. He demands protection from God in the court. God must stop hurting him by withdrawing the "hand," a term meaning to have "control over," and God must prevent Job from being too terrified. If God does these things, then Job will speak and listen. His questions set out his sense of his own victimhood (13:23-25). He insists on being told where he went wrong and why God, who had been his friend, is now his enemy.

swift as a shadow that does not
abide.
³Upon such a one will you set your
eyes,
bringing me into judgment
before you?
⁴Can anyone make the unclean
clean?
No one can.
⁵Since his days are determined—
you know the number of his
months;
you have fixed the limit which
he cannot pass—
⁶Look away from him and let him
be,
while, like a hireling, he com-
pletes his day.
⁷For a tree there is hope;
if it is cut down, it will sprout
again,
its tender shoots will not cease.
⁸Even though its root grow old in
the earth
and its stump die in the dust,
⁹Yet at the first whiff of water it
sprouts
and puts forth branches like a
young plant.

¹⁰But when a man dies, all vigor
leaves him;
when a mortal expires, where
then is he?
¹¹As when the waters of a lake fail,
or a stream shrivels and dries up,
¹²So mortals lie down, never to rise.
Until the heavens are no more,
they shall not awake,
nor be roused out of their sleep.
¹³Oh, that you would hide me in
Sheol,
shelter me till your wrath is past,
fix a time to remember me!
¹⁴If a man were to die, and live again,
all the days of my drudgery I
would wait
for my relief to come.
¹⁵You would call, and I would
answer you;
you would long for the work of
your hands.
¹⁶Surely then you would count my
steps,
and not keep watch for sin in me.
¹⁷My misdeeds would be sealed up
in a pouch,
and you would cover over my
guilt.

He accuses God of placing false legal charges against him, imprisoning him
in the stocks for offenses of long ago, and stalking his footsteps.

The fragility of human life and the hopelessness of the human condition
continue to occupy Job's attention (14:1-22). Job's speeches are the words of
a distraught and broken individual. Their principal logic is the expression of
pain in its multiple aspects, the results of which are circular and repetitive
while Job retells his sorrows again and again. Humans have but a short life,
full of trouble, as ephemeral as a flower or a shadow (14:2). Still addressing God, he wonders why God bothers with such insignificant creatures
as humans. And though Job has just asserted his innocence, he wonders if
any human lives free of some guilt. All Job wants is for God to leave feeble
humanity alone as each one lives out its life of hard labor.

A tree, although it withers and dies, has the possibility of revival, but
when a human dies, nothing is left (14:7-12). Ancient Israel did not believe

¹⁸Mountains fall and crumble,
  rocks move from their place,
¹⁹And water wears away stone,
  and floods wash away the soil
    of the land—
  so you destroy the hope of
    mortals!
²⁰You prevail once for all against
    them and they pass on;
  you dismiss them with changed
    appearance.
²¹If their children are honored, they
    are not aware of it;
  or if disgraced, they do not
    know about them.
²²Only for themselves, their pain;
only for themselves, their
    mourning.

III. Second Cycle of Speeches

15 **Second Speech of Eliphaz.** ¹Then Eliphaz the Temanite answered and said:

²Does a wise man answer with
    windy opinions,
  or puff himself up with the east
    wind?
³Does he argue in speech that does
    not avail,
  and in words that are to no
    profit?

---

in the afterlife of the individual, except in the memory of one's children and in the goodness of one's name, so Job wants his present life to be rich and full, or at least free of his misery. He wishes God would hide him in the underworld until divine anger has passed. He imagines a new beginning when God would call him, esteem him, and stop watching for his misdeeds (14:13-17). But not only are these aspirations merely wishes, they are impossible because God actively prevents a better life with the inevitability of falling rocks or flooding waters (14:17-20). Job may be referring to his sacrifices on behalf of his children (1:5), when he mentions honor or shame of children eluding the parent. All that Job has now is bodily pain and a grieving spirit.

SECOND ROUND OF SPEECHES

Job 15:1–21:34

This cycle of speeches pursues the theme of the fate of the wicked. The friends concentrate on the dire punishment of evildoers, while Job ponders the ways evildoers escape all punishment even as the innocent suffer torment.

15:1-35 Eliphaz's second speech

Although Eliphaz was kind and somewhat gentle in his first speech, he begins his second speech angrily blasting Job for his windy words, airy opinions, and arrogant arguments (15:1-6). Job's speech is dangerous; it does away with "fear of God," here translated "piety" (15:4). Job's own words serve as testimony against him.

⁴You in fact do away with piety,
 you lessen devotion toward God,
⁵Because your wickedness instructs
  your mouth,
 and you choose to speak like the
  crafty.
⁶Your own mouth condemns you,
  not I;
 your own lips refute you.
⁷Were you the first to be born?
 Were you brought forth before
  the hills?
⁸Do you listen in on God's council
 and restrict wisdom to yourself?
⁹What do you know that we do not
  know,
 or understand that we do not?
¹⁰There are gray-haired old men
  among us,
 more advanced in years than
  your father.
¹¹Are the consolations of God not
  enough for you,
 and speech that deals gently
  with you?
¹²Why does your heart carry you
  away,
 and why do your eyes flash,
¹³So that you turn your anger
  against God
 and let such words escape your
  mouth!
¹⁴How can any mortal be blameless,
 anyone born of woman be
  righteous?
¹⁵If in his holy ones God places no
  confidence,
 and if the heavens are not without blame in his sight,
¹⁶How much less so is the abomi-
  nable and corrupt:
 people who drink in iniquity
  like water!
¹⁷I will show you, if you listen to me;
 what I have seen I will tell—
¹⁸What the wise relate

In his second speech, Eliphaz challenges Job's wisdom and responds with "wisdom" of his own. Unlike all previous speeches by the friends, this one does not propose a means of escape. After dismissing Job's words, Eliphaz continues to attack Job's wisdom with a series of questions that undermine Job's authority as a sage (15:7-13). If he was not there at creation, "brought forth before the hills," and if he has not stood in the divine council, how can Job know anything his friends do not know? (15:7-9). The divine council is the heavenly court where God presides over heavenly servants and messengers (Job 1–2). Eliphaz thinks God's consolation should be adequate for Job, perhaps found in Eliphaz's first speech, but Job is not experiencing any such comfort at present. Job is being carried away by false ideas and foolishly voicing anger.

Then, sounding like Job (14:4), Eliphaz exclaims that no one born of a woman's body, that is, humans, can be blameless or righteous. The problem for Eliphaz is probably not women's bodies but the human condition itself. If the holy ones and the heavens are unacceptable to God, all the more lowly is someone who drinks "iniquity," meaning Job himself (15:16).

Eliphaz draws from the established and conventional wisdom of the ancestors about the fate of the wicked in his appeal to get Job to listen

and have not contradicted since
the days of their
ancestors,
¹⁹To whom alone the land was given,
when no foreigner moved
among them:
²⁰The wicked is in torment all his
days,
and limited years are in store for
the ruthless;
²¹The sound of terrors is in his ears;
when all is prosperous, a spoiler
comes upon him.
²²He despairs of escaping the
darkness,
and looks ever for the sword;
²³A wanderer, food for vultures,
he knows destruction is
imminent.
²⁴A day of darkness fills him with
dread;
distress and anguish overpower
him,
like a king expecting an attack.
²⁵Because he has stretched out his
hand against God
and arrogantly challenged the
Almighty,
²⁶Rushing defiantly against him,
with the stout bosses of his
shields.

²⁷Although he has covered his face
with his crassness,
padded his loins with blubber,
²⁸He shall dwell in ruined cities,
in houses that are deserted,
crumbling into rubble.
²⁹He shall not be rich, his possessions shall not endure;
his property shall not spread
over the land.
³⁰A flame shall sear his early growth,
and with the wind his blossoms
shall disappear.
³¹Let him not trust in his height,
misled,
even though his height be like
the palm tree.
³²He shall wither before his time,
his branches no longer green.
³³He shall be like a vine that sheds
its grapes unripened,
like an olive tree casting off its
blossom.
³⁴For the breed of the impious shall
be sterile,
and fire shall consume the tents
of extortioners.
³⁵They conceive malice, bring forth
deceit,
give birth to fraud.

(15:17-35). The speech is a harsh warning to Job, and though Eliphaz has abandoned his more gentle approach from the first speech, and though his own anger at Job seems to be mounting, he surely presents his warning to alter his friend's behavior. The wicked one is in torment and terror for his whole life. And referring directly to Job's situation, Eliphaz declares that destruction comes when "all is prosperous" (15:21). About the wicked, Eliphaz piles up statements of disdain (15:21). They despair, wander, face destruction, become food for vultures, and dread overtakes them. They bring suffering upon themselves by stretching out their hand against the Almighty (15:25). Their fate is to live among ruinous poverty only to die young. Eliphaz confirms the wisdom of his warnings by using proverbial sayings. To clinch his argument, he indirectly compares Job to plants in an environment that yields only barrenness (15:30-35).

16

Job's Fourth Reply. ¹Then Job answered and said:

²I have heard this sort of thing
many times.
Troublesome comforters, all of
you!
³Is there no end to windy words?
What sickness makes you rattle
on?
⁴I also could talk as you do,
were you in my place.
I could declaim over you,
or wag my head at you;
⁵I could strengthen you with talk,
with mere chatter give relief.
⁶If I speak, my pain is not relieved;
if I stop speaking, nothing
changes.
⁷But now he has exhausted me;
you have stunned all my
companions.
⁸You have shriveled me up; it is a
witness,
my gauntness rises up to testify
against me;
⁹His wrath tears and assails me,
he gnashes his teeth against me;
My enemy looks daggers at me.
¹⁰They gape at me with their
mouths;
They strike me on the cheek with
insults;
they are all enlisted against me.
¹¹God has given me over to the
impious;
into the hands of the wicked he
has cast me.
¹²I was in peace, but he dislodged me,
seized me by the neck, dashed
me to pieces.
He has set me up for a target;
¹³his arrows strike me from all
directions.
He pierces my sides without
mercy,
pours out my gall upon the
ground.
¹⁴He pierces me, thrust upon thrust,
rushes at me like a warrior.
¹⁵I have sewn sackcloth on my skin,
laid my horn low in the dust.
¹⁶My face is inflamed with weeping,
darkness covers my eyes,
¹⁷Although my hands are free from
violence,
and my prayer sincere.
¹⁸O earth, do not cover my blood,
nor let my outcry come to rest!
¹⁹Even now my witness is in
heaven,
my advocate is on high.
²⁰My friends it is who wrong me;
before God my eyes shed tears,
²¹That justice may be done for a
mortal with God:
as for a man with his neighbor.
²²For my years are numbered,
and I go the road of no return.

17

¹My spirit is broken, my days
finished,
my burial at hand.
²Surely mockers surround me,
at their provocation, my eyes
grow dim.
³Put up a pledge for me with you:
who is there to give surety for
me?

16:1–17:16 Job's second reply to Eliphaz

Job angrily names the conventional, boring, and useless nature of Eliphaz's advice. But he also admits that were their situations reversed, Job might have spoken in the same "windy" way as his false comforters and presented the same interpretation of suffering as they have (16:1-6). This

⁴You darken their minds to
knowledge;
therefore you will not exalt them.
⁵For a share of property he informs
on friends,
while the eyes of his children
grow dim.
⁶I am made a byword of the people;
I am one at whom people spit.

⁷My eyes are blind with anguish,
and my whole frame is like a
shadow.
⁸The upright are astonished at this,
the innocent aroused against the
wicked.
⁹The righteous holds to his way,
the one with clean hands
increases in strength.

---

acknowledgement underscores Job's pain. His former explanations of misery once shared with his friends no longer fit his life. His pain will not end no matter what words he uses.

Whereas Job's friends blame him for his suffering, Job interprets the cause of his disaster to be God's attacks on him. The betrayal of his friends amplifies his anguish. Verses 7-8 contain grammatical difficulties in the Hebrew, but their general movement is clear. Job laments his devastation and speaks of a witness who betrays him like a wild beast (16:9-10). By verse 11, however, God emerges as Job's betrayer. Job heaps up charges against God with a series of violent verbs, accusing God of handing him over to the wicked, dislodging him from his peace, dashing him to bits, and setting him up as a target. God does these things like a warrior without mercy (16:11-14).

Grief for his own broken life accompanies his anger as he laments his suffering and expresses grief in traditional forms of weeping and wearing sackcloth (16:15-17). The poetry's continual return to Job's grief and vulnerability keeps readers' empathy for him alive by making him a complicated character whose anger at God cannot be easily dismissed as the words of a madman. The interlacing of Job's grief and anger make him human, but his insistence on his innocence, of which readers are aware, makes him a figure of compassion. He suffers at God's hands even though he is innocent (16:17).

Job looks for an ally in the earth itself, personified here as a witness to his suffering (16:18). By commanding the earth not to cover his blood, he appeals to the story of Cain and Abel. There God says to Cain, "your brother's blood cries out to me from the ground" (Gen 4:10; cf. Ezek 24:8). In this poetic way of thinking, blood itself calls for justice as Job begs the ground to keep his cry alive. But the implicit witness of the earth is not enough. Job proclaims he also has a witness in heaven who will speak on his behalf against his friends (16:19). Who this witness might be is not certain. Because Job has just been accusing God of causing his pain, it seems unlikely to be God, although in these verses he admits weeping before God

¹⁰But turn now, and come on again;
      I do not find a wise man among
            you!
¹¹My days pass by, my plans are at
      an end,
      the yearning of my heart.
¹²They would change the night into
      day;
      where there is darkness they
            talk of approaching light.
¹³If my only hope is dwelling in
      Sheol,

and spreading my couch in
      darkness,
¹⁴If I am to say to the pit, "You are
      my father,"
      and to the worm "my mother,"
            "my sister,"
¹⁵Where then is my hope,
      my happiness, who can see it?
¹⁶Will they descend with me into
      Sheol?
      Shall we go down together into
            the dust?

---

and hoping for a just decision in his dispute with his friends. Job's desired witness might be a member of the heavenly council who could argue on his behalf, just as the Satan argued against God in the prologue (chs. 1–2). Or the witness may be the imagined arbiter he wished would stand between him and God in the courtroom (9:33). But Job's hope for justice grows dim because death comes quickly toward him (16:22).

His approaching death continues to haunt him and words about it frame the next chapter (17:1 and 13-16). The imminence of death accentuates his despair, because everything will be over before his world is set right; consequently, justice will elude him. The Hebrew of verses 3-6 is not clear. Job appears to be complaining to God about the wrongful critique his friends are making about him and he appeals for help, for someone to offer "surety" on his behalf. He has no one who will guarantee his innocence, but he appeals to God for such a one anyway (17:3). But then Job claims God is the one who darkens his friends' minds.

To be mocked and turned into a "byword" or popular symbol of brokenness in Job's culture means to be cut off from the community (17:5-6). Job's anguish expands and among his friends he finds only fools who name reality by its opposite (17:11-12). They lie about the world and claim darkness is really approaching light (17:12). As Job resumes his reflections on death, he finds companionship only with corruption and worms that attack the body. These join him with the intimacy of family members on his journey to the nether world. Job's morbid reflections bespeak his hopelessness and isolation in his suffering.

18:1-21 Bildad's second speech

From Bildad's perspective, Job's words appear thoughtless, endless, and harmful. They are self-lacerating and powerless to change either the reality of the earth or the solidity of a rock. Bildad thinks Job has made himself

18 **Bildad's Second Speech.** ¹Then Bildad the Shuhite answered and said:

²When will you put an end to
words?
Reflect, and then we can have
discussion.
³Why are we accounted like beasts,
equal to them in your sight?
⁴You who tear yourself in your
anger—
shall the earth be neglected on
your account
or the rock be moved out of its
place?
⁵Truly, the light of the wicked is
extinguished;
the flame of his fire casts no
light.
⁶In his tent light is darkness;
the lamp above him goes out.
⁷His vigorous steps are hemmed in,
his own counsel casts him down.
⁸A net catches him by the feet,
he wanders into a pitfall.
⁹A trap seizes him by the heel,
a snare lays hold of him.
¹⁰A noose is hidden for him on the
ground,
a netting for him on the path.
¹¹On every side terrors frighten
him;
they harry him at each step.

¹²His strength is famished,
disaster is ready at his side,
¹³His skin is eaten to the limbs,
the firstborn of Death eats his
limbs.
¹⁴He is plucked from the security of
his tent;
and marched off to the king of
terrors.
¹⁵Fire lodges in his tent,
over his abode brimstone is
scattered.
¹⁶Below, his roots dry up,
and above, his branches wither.
¹⁷His memory perishes from the
earth,
and he has no name in the
countryside.
¹⁸He is driven from light into
darkness,
and banished from the world.
¹⁹He has neither offshoot nor
offspring among his people,
no survivor where once he
dwelt.
²⁰Those who come after shall be
appalled at his fate;
those who went before are
seized with horror.
²¹So is it then with the dwelling of
the impious;
such is the place of the one who
does not know God!

---

the center of creation, for Bildad does not understand how profound pain can shrink one's world and alter one's perceptions.

The body of Bildad's speech, however, concerns the fate of the wicked (18:5-21). Like Eliphaz (15:20-25), he presents a frightening picture of the life and death of a person who does not know God (18:21). Perhaps he hopes to terrify Job into altering his speech and changing his attitude, but his didactic approach is harsh and further deepens the alienation between Job and his friends. Like Eliphaz, Bildad fails to mention the bright future toward which his previous speech tried to lead his friend.

19 **Job's Fifth Reply.** ¹Then Job answered and said:

²How long will you afflict my spirit,
grind me down with words?
³These ten times you have
humiliated me,
have assailed me without shame!
⁴Even if it were true that I am at
fault,
my fault would remain with me;
⁵If truly you exalt yourselves at my
expense,
and use my shame as an argument against me,
⁶Know then that it is God who has
dealt unfairly with me,
and compassed me round with
his net.

⁷If I cry out "Violence!" I am not
answered.
I shout for help, but there is no
justice.
⁸He has barred my way and I
cannot pass;
veiled my path in darkness;
⁹He has stripped me of my glory,
taken the diadem from my
brow.
¹⁰He breaks me down on every side,
and I am gone;
he has uprooted my hope like a
tree.
¹¹He has kindled his wrath against
me;
he counts me one of his
enemies.

Imagery of light and darkness creates an envelope around Bildad's depiction of the wicked person (18:5-6 and 18). Bildad asserts that light and harmonious life elude the wicked in their tents. Darkness, here depicted as an encroaching, deathlike force, awaits the evil ones (18:18). The life of the wicked is one of claustrophobic captivity. They are hemmed in and cast down, entrapped and ensnared by nets and a noose. Once captured, the wicked experience more terrifying tortures (18:11-15). Disaster, death's child, and perhaps a reference to disease, stands ready to consume them. Fire destroys the household of the wicked who are like a dried up tree that disappears from memory (see Ps 1:1-3). Because ancient Israelites believed the afterlife of the individual occurred only in the memory of one's children and in the goodness of one's name, the absence of offspring ensures the utter obliteration of the wicked.

All these terrors evoke Job's own condition. He is covered in sores (2:7-8) and his children are dead (17:18-19). No one will remember him and his spirit is dried up. Bildad's vivid accounting of the destiny of the wicked speaks of Job indirectly, but no less transparently, as the wicked one whose fate will appall later generations.

19:1-29 Job's second reply to Bildad

Job begins with the now-expected criticism of the previous speaker (19:2-4). Using a phrase common in lament psalms, he asks no one in particular, "How long?" How long will his friends continue to assault him and endlessly revile him "without shame." In the central section of Job's reply,

¹²His troops advance as one;
  they build up their road to
    attack me,
  encamp around my tent.
¹³My family has withdrawn from
    me,
  my friends are wholly estranged.
¹⁴My relatives and companions
    neglect me,
  my guests have forgotten me.
¹⁵Even my maidservants consider
    me a stranger;
  I am a foreigner in their sight.
¹⁶I call my servant, but he gives no
    answer,
  though I plead aloud with him.
¹⁷My breath is abhorrent to my wife;
  I am loathsome to my very
    children.
¹⁸Even young children despise me;
  when I appear, they speak
    against me.

¹⁹All my intimate friends hold me
    in horror;
  those whom I loved have turned
    against me!
²⁰My bones cling to my skin,
  and I have escaped by the skin
    of my teeth.
²¹Pity me, pity me, you my friends,
  for the hand of God has struck
    me!
²²Why do you pursue me like God,
  and prey insatiably upon me?
²³Oh, would that my words were
    written down!
  Would that they were inscribed
    in a record:
²⁴That with an iron chisel and with
    lead
  they were cut in the rock
    forever!
²⁵As for me, I know that my
    vindicator lives,

---

however, he speaks of his suffering life in terms that parallel and expand Bildad's depiction of the fate of the wicked (19:5-22). The two friends see the reality of Job's suffering but draw radically different interpretations from it. In Job's view, he suffers not because he is wicked, but because God is unfair (19:3). He does not address God in this speech as he has in every speech before. Instead, he speaks to his friends (19:1-6, 21-22, 28-29) and complains to them about God's treatment of him in their triangulated relationship (19:6-12).

Job's complaint shows him to be an angry, grieving person who cannot find enough ways to describe his experiences of claustrophobia and hopelessness. If his friends continue to reproach him, they should know it is God who "has dealt unfairly" with him and trapped him with a net (19:6). In Job's interpretation of his suffering, God is the active agent who initiates all his mistreatment and, like his friends, gives no hearing to Job's cries of "violence" (some translations read "injustice"). In a depiction of his life that echoes Bildad's speech, Job piles up accusations against God who bars his way, puts darkness across his path, strips him of glory, treats him like an enemy, and sends disciplined, unified troops against him (19:7-12). To Job, God resembles a military commander who sends unnamed forces to attack him.

and that he will at last stand
forth upon the dust.
²⁶This will happen when my skin
has been stripped off,
and from my flesh I will see God:
²⁷I will see for myself,
my own eyes, not another's, will
behold him:
my inmost being is consumed
with longing.

²⁸But you who say, "How shall we
persecute him,
seeing that the root of the matter
is found in him?"
²⁹Be afraid of the sword for yourselves,
for your anger is a crime
deserving the sword;
that you may know that there is
a judgment.

Job then shifts the focus of his lament from God to companions who have betrayed and abandoned him (19:13-22). He lists friends, servants, wife, and other members of his extended household—all his "intimate friends hold [him] in horror" (19:19). He feels the heartbreaking pain of abandonment and isolation, made all the more torturous because it is his closest friends and intimate members of his household who have betrayed him. In a verse difficult to translate, he complains that his own body turns against him as he wastes away and has escaped only "by the skin of my teeth," as some translations put it (19:20; NRSV). Whatever the Hebrew means, it is part of the evidence of God's attack on him and one reason he begs his arrogant friends to pity him (19:21-22).

Though death may be near, Job is not dead yet. Laments in the prayer of ancient Israel often turn from complaint to an act of hope, to wishing for someone who would vindicate the speaker so that the present situation would not be the last word (19:23-29). Job wants his own lament to be chiseled in stone as a permanent record of his innocence, a kind of witness on his behalf. But he also wants a redeemer, translated here as "vindicator," one who will legally establish his innocence. He wants to be declared blameless in his "flesh," that is, in his own body with his "own eyes" before his death. In these dramatic verses Job affirms that his "vindicator lives" (19:25).

The Hebrew title translated "vindicator" is a legal one and refers to the "redeemer" who buys back kinfolk from slavery, pays their debts, and buys back land taken by creditors (cf. Lev 25:23-24, 47-55; Deut 25:5-10). Some interpreters think Job's vindicator personifies his own cry, witnessing on his behalf. Others propose that Job seeks someone who can act as a mediator between himself and God (cf. 9:33; 16:19). Still others think Job expresses faith that the redeemer is God who will judge him to be innocent. However one understands Job's redeemer, the desire to "see God" consumes Job with longing, for only God can declare him in the right (19:26). Though later Christian tradition finds hope for personal resurrection in this verse,

Zophar's Second Speech. ¹Then Zophar the Naamathite answered and said:

²So now my thoughts provide an
answer for me,
because of the feelings within
me.
³A rebuke that puts me to shame I
hear,
and from my understanding a
spirit gives me a reply.
⁴Do you not know this: from of old,
since human beings were placed
upon the earth,
⁵The triumph of the wicked is short
and the joy of the impious but
for a moment?
⁶Though his pride mount up to the
heavens
and his head reach to the clouds,
⁷Yet he perishes forever like the
dung he uses for fuel,
and onlookers say, "Where is
he?"
⁸Like a dream he takes flight and
cannot be found;
he fades away like a vision of
the night.
⁹The eye which saw him does so no
more;
nor shall his dwelling again
behold him.
¹⁰His sons will restore to the poor,

and his hands will yield up his
riches.
¹¹Though his bones are full of
youthful vigor,
it shall lie with him in the dust.
¹²Though wickedness is sweet in his
mouth,
and he hides it under his tongue,
¹³Though he retains it and will not
let it go
but keeps it still within his
mouth,
¹⁴Yet in his stomach the food shall
turn;
it shall be venom of asps inside
him.
¹⁵The riches he swallowed he shall
vomit up;
God shall make his belly
disgorge them.
¹⁶The poison of asps he shall drink
in;
the viper's fangs shall slay him.
¹⁷He shall see no streams of oil,
no torrents of honey or milk.
¹⁸He shall give back his gains, never
used;
like his profit from trade, never
enjoyed.
¹⁹Because he has oppressed and
neglected the poor,
and stolen a house he did not
build;

ancient Israel did not believe in the afterlife of the individual until the very end of the Old Testament period (see 14:10-22).

Job ends his speech by quoting his friends who find the problem to be him, and he warns them of judgment to come (19:28-29).

20:1-29 Zophar's second speech

Rebuking speech introduces the words of a new speaker. The purpose of these reproaches is to counter the authority of the previous speaker, in this case, of Job (20:2-3). Zophar claims Job has provoked him and thereby enabled him to understand Job's plight. After these words, readers might expect Zophar's counsel to take a new direction, since this is the only remark

²⁰For he has known no quiet in his
greed,
in his treasure he cannot save
himself.
²¹None of his survivors will
consume it,
therefore his prosperity shall not
endure.
^{22c}When he has more than enough,
distress shall be his,
every sort of trouble shall come
upon him.
²³When he has filled his belly,
God shall send against him the
fury of his wrath

and rain down his missiles upon
him.
²⁴Should he escape an iron weapon,
a bronze bow shall pierce him
through;
²⁵The dart shall come out of his back,
a shining point out of his
gall-bladder:
terrors fall upon him.
²⁶Complete darkness is in store for
his treasured ones;
a fire unfanned shall consume
him;
any survivor in his tent shall be
destroyed.

---

by one of Job's friends to indicate someone is actually listening to him. But like Eliphaz and Bildad before him, Zophar devotes his second speech to a dramatic depiction of the fate of the wicked. His words reveal his growing frustration with Job and his deepening belief in Job's guilt. Unlike his previous speech, he offers no advice to his friend on how to escape his predicament (11:14-19). His words merely warn Job that his present course leads to greater calamity.

The torments awaiting the guilty occupy Zophar's imagination. Four times he names God as the one who enacts the torture due to the wicked (20:15, 23, 28, 29). On this point, he seems to agree with Job's view of God, but Zophar thinks God is justified in tormenting people. Job claims he is innocent and God tortures him anyway (19:3-12). By contrast to the brutal power of God, the wicked are ephemeral beings, according to Zophar. They perish like the "dung he uses for fuel" and fade like "a vision of the night," finally to disappear from the human community (20:6-8).

Outward appearances of the wicked are deceptive (20:11-19). They seem to be healthy and vigorous, hiding wickedness under their tongues, that is, under wise and appropriate speech, and they may be rich as well. But wickedness resides inside them like a poison gaining dominion over their bodies. God will intervene to force the disgorgement of riches like food from a poisoned stomach. And even if the wicked enjoy some benefits in life, they experience no joy.

Zophar's accusations identify specific evil deeds among actions of the wicked; they oppress the poor (20:19). The Hebrew, however, specifies that oppression more strongly as the crushing and abandoning of the poor and

²⁷The heavens shall reveal his guilt,
  and the earth rise up against him.
²⁸The flood shall sweep away his
    house,
  torrents in the day of God's
    anger.
²⁹This is the portion of the wicked,
  the heritage appointed him by
    God.

21 **Job's Sixth Reply.** ¹Then Job an-
    swered and said:

²At least listen to my words,
  and let that be the consolation
    you offer.

³Bear with me while I speak;
  and after I have spoken, you can
    mock!
⁴Is my complaint toward any
    human being?
  Why should I not be impatient?
⁵Look at me and be appalled,
  put your hands over your
    mouths.
⁶When I think of it, I am dismayed,
  and shuddering seizes my flesh.
⁷Why do the wicked keep on
    living,
  grow old, become mighty in
    power?

as the violent taking possession of a house that the wicked did not build. These acts of treachery result from greed; therefore, the wealth of the wicked will provide no respite (20:21-22). Nor can the wealth of the sinner be interpreted as a sign of divine blessing, as many in the ancient world believed. Instead, for Zophar, wealth is as the sign of devious and evil dealings so it will neither endure nor save (20:20-22).

Beyond lack of enjoyment of the good life, the wicked will experience horrific torments whose originating source is the fury of God (20:23-29). The NABRE and other translations supply the word "God" as the subject of verse 23, but the text uses the pronoun "he" and reveals who "he" is only in the last word (20:29). The effect of withholding the identity of the attacker until the poem's end is shock, since the assault upon the wicked is vicious. Though the Hebrew of verse 23 is unclear, it is clear that the attacker will rain down fury upon the guilty, bring weapons of war against them, set them in darkness, and consume them in fire. The cosmos will conspire against the wicked and reveal their guilt. Floods of anger will sweep them away. The last line of Zophar's speech names these disasters as the "portion" and "heritage" of the wicked, reversing traditional understandings of these terms as divine blessings. Zophar presents a bleak future for Job, whom he assumes to be among those he has been describing.

21:1-34 Job's second reply to Zophar

Job closes this cycle of speeches by responding to his friends' accounts of the fate of the wicked, often alluding to their speeches. He speaks directly to them in this chapter and neither calls upon God nor engages in a long

⁸Their progeny is secure in their
    sight;
    their offspring are before their
        eyes.
⁹Their homes are safe, without fear,
    and the rod of God is not upon
        them.
¹⁰Their bulls breed without fail;
    their cows calve and do not
        miscarry.
¹¹They let their young run free like
    sheep,
    their children skip about.
¹²They sing along with drum and
    lyre,
    and make merry to the sound of
        the pipe.

¹³They live out their days in
    prosperity,
    and tranquilly go down to Sheol.
¹⁴Yet they say to God, "Depart from
    us,
    for we have no desire to know
        your ways!
¹⁵What is the Almighty that we
    should serve him?
    And what do we gain by
        praying to him?"
¹⁶Their happiness is not in their
    own hands.
    The designs of the wicked are
        far from me!
¹⁷How often is the lamp of the
    wicked put out?

---

monologue. Job interprets the destinies of the innocent and the wicked quite differently from his friends. He thinks it is shocking that the wicked get away with their crimes, live abundantly, and go to the grave after a life of contentment. He wants to know why.

Job begins by demanding what he needs from his friends (21:1-6). He needs them to "listen." His friends should be able to "bear with" him as he describes his life. Were they able to hear him, he could find comfort. If they listened, they would be able to see his deep pain from his point of view, even if they did not agree with him. If they listened, they would accord him personal dignity and honor, and, like him, they too would be horrified.

Job shows in this speech that he has been listening to them. He responds to their understanding of the wicked and the just punishment the friends believe they receive. Job asks a question to show his perspective: "Why do the wicked keep on living, grow old, become mighty in power?" (21:7). Job does not answer his own question, but instead sets up the opposite case in rhythmic parallel sentences (21:8-16). Their offspring are secure, their homes peaceful, and God's punishment is absent from their lives. Even their cattle thrive, and their children are healthy, safe, and happy. The wicked and their families sing, dance, and make merry; then they die in peace. No harm seems to come to these people. Yet despite the evident harmony of their lives, they have turned from God and deserve none of these blessings. The text quotes them to reveal the depth of their sin. They are adamantly alienated from God, deny the Almighty's power, and refuse to serve (21:14-15).

How often does destruction
come upon them,
the portion God allots in his
anger?
¹⁸Let them be like straw before the
wind,
like chaff the storm carries
away!
¹⁹"God is storing up the man's
misery for his children"?—
let him requite the man himself
so that he knows it!
²⁰Let his own eyes behold his
calamity,
and the wrath of the Almighty
let him drink!
²¹For what interest has he in his
family after him,
when the number of his months
is finished?
²²Can anyone teach God
knowledge,
seeing that he judges those on
high?
²³One dies in his full vigor,
wholly at ease and content;
²⁴His figure is full and nourished,
his bones are moist with marrow.
²⁵Another dies with a bitter spirit,
never having tasted happiness.

²⁶Alike they lie down in the dust,
and worms cover them both.
²⁷See, I know your thoughts,
and the arguments you plot
against me.
²⁸For you say, "Where is the house
of the great,
and where the dwelling place of
the wicked?"
²⁹Have you not asked the wayfarers
and do you not acknowledge
the witness they give?
³⁰On the day of calamity the evil
man is spared,
on the day that wrath is
released.
³¹Who will charge him to his face
about his conduct,
and for what he has done who
will repay him?
³²He is carried to the grave
and at his tomb they keep watch.
³³Sweet to him are the clods of the
valley.
All humankind will follow after
him,
and countless others before him.
³⁴How empty the consolation you
offer me!
Your arguments remain a fraud.

Job's observations contradict the reigning beliefs of his friends who hold that sin affects one's entire family, especially offspring. Job now asks how often the wicked pay for their sins? (21:17). In his view, they escape suffering and avoid just punishment. He utters curses against them, hoping for God to do justice by punishing the sinner and not deferring it to the children (21:18-21). Like Ecclesiastes, Job maintains that there is no justice because death treats the good and the bad alike (Eccl 3:16-20).

This cycle of speeches concludes with Job's challenge to his friends (21:27-34). He knows they think he is wicked, but the real evildoers go unchallenged. Because his friends are completely wrong about God's distribution of suffering among the wicked and the innocent, they can offer Job no comfort. And, Job adds, they are unreliable because of the duplicity of their speech (21:34).

IV. Third Cycle of Speeches

22 **Eliphaz's Third Speech.** ¹Then Eliphaz the Temanite answered and said:

²Can a man be profitable to God?
  Can a wise man be profitable to
    him?
³Does it please the Almighty that
    you are just?
  Does he gain if your ways are
    perfect?
⁴Is it because of your piety that he
    reproves you—
  that he enters into judgment
    with you?
⁵Is not your wickedness great,
    your iniquity endless?
⁶You keep your relatives' goods in
    pledge unjustly,
  leave them stripped naked of
    their clothing.
⁷To the thirsty you give no water to
    drink,
  and from the hungry you with-
    hold bread;
⁸As if the land belonged to the
    powerful,
  and only the privileged could
    dwell in it!
⁹You sent widows away empty-
    handed,
  and the resources of orphans are
    destroyed.
¹⁰Therefore snares are round about
    you,
  sudden terror makes you panic,
¹¹Or darkness—you cannot see!
  A deluge of waters covers you.

THIRD ROUND OF SPEECHES

Job 22:1–31:40

The final round of speeches among the friends differs from the previous two in a number of ways and disrupts patterns established there. The speeches of Eliphaz and Bildad are much shorter than their previous discourses, while Zophar has no speech at all. By contrast, Job's last speech in reply to Bildad is the longest in the book (chs. 26–31). Surprisingly, in these chapters Job often appears to take up the positions of his three friends. Interpreters explain these features in a variety of ways. Some interpreters believe the text was disrupted when it was copied, omitting Zophar's speech and parts of the others. Some think editors added material to Job's speech, namely chapter 28.

In the book's present form, however, alterations in the previous arrangement of speeches probably imply a great deal more than editorial error or addition. If the present arrangement is deliberate rather than chance confusion and disorder, then the shortening of the friends' words and the increase in Job's words provokes reflection on the debate. On the one hand, the friends' words have lost their power. Lacking further creative insight, their speech fades away as if their point of view has come to an impasse. Job's words, on the other hand, grow in length and authority, revealing increasing strength. His character has changed across the book from the one

¹²Does not God, in the heights of
the heavens,
behold the top of the stars, high
though they are?
¹³Yet you say, "What does God
know?
Can he judge through the thick
darkness?
¹⁴Clouds hide him so that he cannot
see
as he walks around the circuit of
the heavens!"
¹⁵Do you indeed keep to the ancient
way
trodden by the worthless?
¹⁶They were snatched before their
time;
their foundations a river swept
away.
¹⁷They said to God, "Let us alone!"
and, "What can the Almighty do
to us?"
¹⁸Yet he had filled their houses with
good things.
The designs of the wicked are
far from me!
¹⁹The just look on and are glad,
and the innocent deride them:
²⁰"Truly our enemies are destroyed,
and what was left to them, fire
has consumed!"
²¹Settle with him and have peace.
That way good shall come to
you:

who wanted to die (ch. 3) and for whom words were futile and inadequate (9:20-12), and who knew only terror before God (9:3-15) to become, in his final speech, a forceful, potent spokesperson on his own behalf.

When Job espouses aspects of his friends' arguments, he is probably employing a device known in Babylonian literature where an opponent takes up the opposite position so no point of view completely triumphs over the other. In this way, the book of Job invites readers to take competing interpretations of Job's suffering with equal seriousness and to struggle with his dilemma.

22:1-30 Eliphaz's third speech

Clearly, Eliphaz was not moved by Job's previous appeals to his friends to listen to him. Eliphaz begins with a series of rhetorical questions about human relationship with God (22:2-5). The questions start innocently with humanity in general, but then move to accuse Job of "great" wickedness (22:2-5).

In Eliphaz's understanding, God is unmoved by human self-worth or by their efforts to be just and pious. Self-sufficient and detached from humans, God's judgments are fair and impartial. The questions addressed to Job in second person singular ask him if it is not his own doing that God has brought judgment upon him (22:3b-5).

From these unforgiving but general questions, Eliphaz turns to attack Job directly (22:6-18). First, he accuses Job of injustice (22:6-9). Job, he claims, has wrongly garnered the goods of poor kinfolk, stripped them of clothing, withheld water and nourishment from the hungry, and failed to aid widows

²²Receive instruction from his mouth,
and place his words in your
heart.
²³If you return to the Almighty, you
will be restored;
if you put iniquity far from your
tent,
²⁴And treat raw gold as dust,
the fine gold of Ophir as pebbles
in the wadi,
²⁵Then the Almighty himself shall
be your gold
and your sparkling silver.
²⁶For then you shall delight in the
Almighty,
you shall lift up your face
toward God.
²⁷Entreat him and he will hear you,
and your vows you shall fulfill.

²⁸What you decide shall succeed for
you,
and upon your ways light shall
shine.
²⁹For when they are brought low,
you will say, "It is pride!"
But downcast eyes he saves.
³⁰He will deliver whoever is
innocent;
you shall be delivered if your
hands are clean.

23 **Job's Seventh Reply.** ¹Then Job
answered and said:

²Today especially my complaint is
bitter,
his hand is heavy upon me in
my groanings.

and orphans. These sins involve attacks on the poor and those without protection in the society. Such actions grievously violate torah and covenant relations in Israel. Job's sins against the poor have led to his misery (22:10-11). But Eliphaz fabricates these charges against Job, for readers know that Job is "blameless and upright"; he "feared God and avoided evil" (1:1). Eliphaz must be motivated to this extreme misreading of Job's life because, if Job is innocent, then Eliphaz's own worldview, his understanding of God, and his sense of his place in the world would collapse upon him.

Instead of listening to Job, Eliphaz hurries to defend God. He asks Job if God is not higher than the heavens, to which Job would surely reply "yes." Then, having set Job up, he accuses him of turning from God. He quotes words Job has not spoken, claiming that clouds and darkness blind God's just judgment. But Job accused God of seeing well his innocence and deliberately distorting justice (9:20; 10:7). In Eliphaz's view, Job acts wickedly just like Noah's generation (22:16; cf. Gen 6).

Eliphaz makes one more appeal to his friend to repent and turn back to the Almighty (22:21-30). Assuming Job's guilt, Eliphaz promises goodness and restored relationship between Job and God will follow Job's repentance. The choice is in his hands. If he turns to God and rejects iniquity, then life will be good again, "light shall shine" (22:28). Eliphaz sums up his theology that God delivers the innocent with more proverbial instruction (22:30). Through spiritual practices, Job can save himself.

³Would that I knew how to find him,
that I might come to his dwelling!
⁴I would set out my case before
him,
fill my mouth with arguments;
⁵I would learn the words he would
answer me,
understand what he would say
to me.
⁶Would he contend against me with
his great power?
No, he himself would heed me!
⁷There an upright man might argue
with him,
and I would once and for all be
delivered from my judge.
⁸But if I go east, he is not there;
or west, I cannot perceive him;
⁹The north enfolds him, and I can-
not catch sight of him;
The south hides him, and I cannot see him.
¹⁰Yet he knows my way;
if he tested me, I should come
forth like gold.
¹¹My foot has always walked in his
steps;
I have kept his way and not
turned aside.
¹²From the commands of his lips I
have not departed;
the words of his mouth I have
treasured in my heart.

¹³But once he decides, who can con-
tradict him?
What he desires, that he does.
¹⁴For he will carry out what is ap-
pointed for me,
and many such things he has in
store.
¹⁵Therefore I am terrified before
him;
when I take thought, I dread
him.
¹⁶For it is God who has made my
heart faint,
the Almighty who has terrified
me.
¹⁷Yes, would that I had vanished in
darkness,
hidden by the thick gloom before me.

24 ¹Why are times not set by the
Almighty,
and why do his friends not see
his days?
²People remove landmarks;
they steal herds and pasture
them.
³The donkeys of orphans they drive
away;
they take the widow's ox for a
pledge.
⁴They force the needy off the road;
all the poor of the land are
driven into hiding.

23:1–24:25 Job's third reply to Eliphaz

Despite Eliphaz's efforts to change his friend, Job grows stronger in his own interpretation of his predicament. He wants to meet the Almighty in a courtroom (23:3-6). Legal metaphors reappear in his speech (9:13-21; 13:14-27) as he pictures himself at trial. He imagines God hearing and receiving his arguments. God and he would have a reasonable exchange, and though the Hebrew of verse seven is unclear, Job clearly anticipates an outcome of justice, of gaining his rights (23:7).

But his present experience of God's absence dampens confidence in a just legal outcome (23:8). God is nowhere to be found, although Job searches

⁵Like wild donkeys in the
wilderness,
they go forth to their task of
seeking prey;
the steppe provides food for
their young;
⁶They harvest fodder in the field,
and glean in the vineyard of the
wicked.
⁷They pass the night naked,
without clothing;
they have no covering against
the cold;
⁸They are drenched with rain from
the mountains,
and for want of shelter they
cling to the rock.
⁹Orphans are snatched from the
breast,
infants of the needy are taken in
pledge.
¹⁰They go about naked, without
clothing,
and famished, they carry the
sheaves.

¹¹Between the rows they press out
the oil;
they tread the wine presses, yet
are thirsty.
¹²In the city the dying groan,
and the souls of the wounded
cry out.
Yet God does not treat it as a
disgrace!
¹³They are rebels against the light:
they do not recognize its ways;
they do not stay in its paths.
¹⁴When there is no light the
murderer rises,
to kill the poor and needy;
in the night he acts like a thief.
¹⁵The eye of the adulterer watches
for the twilight;
he says, "No eye will see me."
He puts a mask over his face;
¹⁶in the dark he breaks into
houses;
By day they shut themselves in;
they do not know the light.

---

in every direction. He uses the compass points to lament divine absence, hidden from him no matter how hard he searches. In the next verses (23:10-12), he reasserts his belief that God knows he is innocent (cf. 10:7) and reiterates his claim that he has lived in constant fidelity, treasuring God's word in his inmost being (cf. 13:15). The problem in their relationship lies with God (23:13-17). No matter the injustice of divine decisions, God cannot be challenged (23:13-14). When he thinks of God, Job lives in conflict between hope and despair, but despair seems stronger (23:17).

Job reflects on the fate of the wicked, the subject that has dominated speeches in this cycle, but here Job also considers the fate of their victims. He yearns for God to set times, presumably for justice, and for God to make them visible. Instead, the wicked steal property by moving landmarks and steal people's livelihoods. They feed on the orphans, widows, and the poor. The poor, in turn, are forced into the wilderness to lead onerous, dangerous lives, exposed to the elements and enslaved to the wicked. And, observes Job, God does not act on their behalf, even though they are dying in the dust (23:12).

[17]Indeed, for all of them morning is
  deep darkness;
    then they recognize the terrors
      of deep darkness.
[18]He is swift on the surface of the
  water:
    their portion in the land is
      accursed,
    they do not turn aside by way of
      the vineyards.
[19]Drought and heat snatch away the
  snow waters,
    Sheol, those who have sinned.
[20]May the womb forget him,
  may the worm find him sweet,
    may he no longer be
      remembered;
And may wickedness be broken
  like a tree.
[21]May his companion be barren,
  unable to give birth,
    may his widow not prosper!
[22]He sustains the mighty by his
  strength,
    to him who rises without
      assurance of his life
[23]he gives safety and support,
and his eyes are on their ways.
[24]They are exalted for a while, and
  then are no more;
    laid low, like everyone else they
      are gathered up;
    like ears of grain they shrivel.
[25]If this be not so, who can make me
  a liar,
    and reduce my words to nothing?

25 Bildad's Third Speech. [1]Then Bildad the Shuhite answered and said:

[2]Dominion and dread are his
  who brings about harmony in
    his heavens.
[3]Is there any numbering of his
  troops?
    Yet on which of them does his
      light not rise?
[4]How can anyone be in the right
  against God,
    or how can any born of woman
      be innocent?
[5]Even the moon is not bright
  and the stars are not clean in his
    eyes.

Imagery of light and darkness dramatizes Job's perceptions of the good and the wicked (24:13-20). The wicked rebel against the light, against wisdom and right relationship with God and humans. They commit all kinds of evil in the dark, treating time as the domain of wickedness. They hide from light and roam about in darkness. The powerful seem to have God on their side, but ultimately they disappear. Of course, that may be a long time in the future, but Job thinks his words are irrefutable.

25:1-6 Bildad's third speech

Bildad concludes with a hymnic appreciation of divine power (25:1-3) contrasted with the lowly state of humanity (25:4-6). His words present major opinions of the friends and act as a succinct summary of their theological positions on Job's messy life. He views God as the creator who brings about harm and peace in a mythic battle against chaos. He affirms his friends' sense of the world as a static place, evident in the order of the heavens and sure to be enacted on earth. Before such a powerful God, what

⁶How much less a human being,
    who is but a worm,
    a mortal, who is only a maggot?

26 **Job's Reply.** ¹Then Job answered
and said:

²What help you give to the power-
    less,
    what strength to the feeble arm!
³How you give counsel to one with-
    out wisdom;

how profuse is the advice you
    offer!
⁴With whose help have you uttered
    those words,
    whose breath comes forth from
    you?
⁵The shades beneath writhe in terror,
    the waters, and their inhabitants.
⁶Naked before him is Sheol,
    and Abaddon has no covering.
⁷He stretches out Zaphon over the
    void,

---

human can be judged to be righteous? No human, born of woman, can be pure if even the moon and stars are not clear before God (25:4).

Bildad's reference to women and childbirth is probably not a negative comment on womanhood so much as it insists that humans are mere mortals who participate in the cycle of birth and death over and against divine awesomeness. But Bildad's view of humanity is dismal, indeed, for humans are no better than maggots and worms (25:6). His friends share this point of view (4:17-21; 11:11; 15:14-16; 22:2-3). Humans are hopelessly trapped in their situation and cannot expect justice before God. This perspective conflicts with another view consistent among them that Job is at fault for his own transgressions, hidden and not so hidden. He has power to escape his suffering, if he would only turn to God (5:8; 8:5-7; 11:13-14; 22:21-30).

26:1–31:40 Job's final reply

Job's last speech to his friends comprises six chapters, though many interpreters subdivide it because it contains a variety of literary forms and themes. Job begins typically enough, complaining to his friends and questioning God's abusive power (26:1–27:21), but in chapter 28, he changes both his subject and the genre of his discourse. Called a hymn to Wisdom, chapter 28 appears to interrupt Job's tone, because it is tranquil and hopeful. Many interpreters think it was simply inserted here by a later writer and not an original part of Job's speech. In the next three chapters, Job laments his lost past (ch. 29), complains about the bitter present (ch. 30), and utters oaths asserting his innocence. Together these chapters mount Job's self-defense as if he is in a divorce court where one partner is betrayed by the unfaithfulness of the other. He insists that God name the charges against him (ch. 31). The text unifies disparate poetic pieces into one bumpy whole that expresses Job's anger and doubt along with his last grasp at hope. Perhaps Job's defense functions in the book to draw God forth from hiding.

and suspends the earth over
nothing at all;
⁸He binds up the waters in his
clouds,
yet the cloud is not split by their
weight;
⁹He holds back the appearance of
the full moon
by spreading his clouds before it.
¹⁰He has marked out a circle on the
surface of the deep
as the boundary of light and
darkness.
¹¹The pillars of the heavens tremble
and are stunned at his
thunderous rebuke;
¹²By his power he stilled Sea,
by his skill he crushed Rahab;
¹³By his wind the heavens were
made clear,
his hand pierced the fleeing ser-
pent.
¹⁴Lo, these are but the outlines of
his ways,
and what a whisper of a word
we hear of him:
Who can comprehend the
thunder of his power?

27 **Job's Reply.** ¹Job took up his
theme again and said:

²As God lives, who takes away my
right,
the Almighty, who has made my
life bitter,
³So long as I still have life breath in
me,
the breath of God in my nostrils,

⁴My lips shall not speak falsehood,
nor my tongue utter deceit!
⁵Far be it from me to account you
right;
till I die I will not renounce my
innocence.
⁶My justice I maintain and I will not
relinquish it;
my heart does not reproach me
for any of my days.
⁷Let my enemy be as the wicked
and my adversary as the unjust!
⁸For what hope has the impious
when he is cut off,
when God requires his life?
⁹Will God then listen to his cry
when distress comes upon him,
¹⁰If he delights in the Almighty
and calls upon God constantly?
¹¹I will teach you what is in God's
hand,
and the way of the Almighty I
will not conceal.
¹²Look, you yourselves have all
seen it;
why do you spend yourselves in
empty words!
¹³This is the portion of the wicked
with God,
the heritage oppressors receive
from the Almighty:
¹⁴Though his children be many, the
sword awaits them.
His descendants shall want for
bread.
¹⁵His survivors shall be buried in
death;
their widows shall not weep.

26:1–27:21 Job's reply to his friends

Job begins sarcastically, demanding an explanation of his friends' words to help the "powerless," namely himself. Their counsel is insulting, verbose, and without wisdom. Since wisdom in Israel attends to human experience, they have failed in their role as wise elders and friends because they have disdained his words about his experience.

¹⁶Though he heap up silver like
dust
and store away mounds of
clothing,
¹⁷What he has stored the righteous
shall wear,
and the innocent shall divide
the silver.
¹⁸He builds his house as of cobwebs,
or like a booth put up by a
watchman.
¹⁹He lies down a rich man, one last
time;

he opens his eyes—nothing is
there.
²⁰Terrors flood over him like water,
at night the tempest carries him
off.
²¹The east wind seizes him and he is
gone;
it sweeps him from his place;
²²It hurls itself at him without pity,
as he tries to flee from its power.
²³It claps its hands at him,
and whistles at him from its
place.

Some interpreters think the next verses (26:5-14) actually belong to Bildad since they pick up creation language Bildad uses (25:5). When Job has
spoken of creation before (9:5-13; 10:8-3; 12:13-25), he has portrayed it as
chaotic and evidence of God's lack of justice and wisdom. Job seems to offer
a more orderly view of "the outlines of [God's] ways" than is characteristic
of him (26:14). But if that is so, Job may be using a tactic of ancient argument that presents the opponents' views in order to keep any one perspective from complete domination in the debate. Yet Job echoes themes and
language in this chapter that he used in the hymn in chapter nine (9:4-13).

To whomever the verses should be ascribed, they contain beautiful
imagery arising from ancient Near Eastern creation myths. The underworld, known both as Sheol and Abaddon, lies open and exposed before
the powerful deity. The earth and the North, mythic realms of the gods,
hang in space. The Creator controls the rain and the clouds and marks out
light and dark in a circle. The created world and the pillars upon which the
world is set tremble as God rebukes them.

Job's account of creation exalts divine power against the sea monster
Rahab and the dragon, the mythic figures of chaos (26:12). Angry storms
heed God's design. The Creator is powerful and magnificent. Job's words
laud that power of combat against sea monsters, hidden from humans,
and cause of fear. This stirring hymn is not completely alien to Job's way
of speaking.

The introduction to chapter 27, "Job took up his theme again," smoothes
out the interrupting boundary between this chapter and the previous chapter. After chiding his friends and promising to teach them God's ways, Job
uses the oath, "as God lives," to declare his innocence with solemnity and

V. The Poem on Wisdom

28 Where Is Wisdom to be Found?

¹There is indeed a mine for silver,
and a place for refining gold.
²Iron is taken from the earth,
and copper smelted out of stone.
³He sets a boundary for the
darkness;
the farthest confines he explores.
⁴He breaks open a shaft far from
habitation,
unknown to human feet;
suspended, far from people,
they sway.
⁵The earth, though out of it comes
forth bread,
is in fiery upheaval underneath.
⁶Its stones are the source of lapis
lazuli,
and there is gold in its dust.

⁷The path no bird of prey knows,
nor has the hawk's eye seen it.
⁸The proud beasts have not trodden
it,
nor has the lion gone that way.
⁹He sets his hand to the flinty rock,
and overturns the mountains at
their root.
¹⁰He splits channels in the rocks;
his eyes behold all that is
precious.
¹¹He dams up the sources of the
streams,
and brings hidden things to light.
¹²As for wisdom—where can she be
found?
Where is the place of understanding?
¹³Mortals do not know her path,
nor is she to be found in the
land of the living.

---

to stake his innocence in the highest authority (27:1-6). He cannot agree with his friends and promises to maintain his innocence with a clear conscience until death.

The fate of the wicked reappears, and Job turns the criticism against his friends who, with their "empty words," are his implied enemy (27:7-21). This is where he begins to sound like his friends because he agrees that God will punish the wicked while the just will prevail in the long run (26:17). Some interpreters believe these words are the missing final speech of Zophar, yet the text assigns them to Job. These words may again follow the practice of some ancient Near Eastern texts of assigning the opponent's viewpoint to the final speaker. Borrowing imagery from Bildad (8:14), Job claims the houses of the wicked are no more sturdy than "cobwebs" (27:18). Storms will sweep the wicked away. These last lines anticipate the storm in which Job meets God, though different vocabulary appears there and no one is swept away (38:1).

Job 28:1-28 Hymn to wisdom

The problems of this chapter become immediately apparent to any careful reader. Job changes the subject from his suffering and the fate of the wicked in the previous speeches to the search for wisdom. The tone of the passage changes, too, from discontent to tranquility. It ends with a

¹⁴The Deep says, "She is not in me";
and the Sea says, "She is not
with me."
¹⁵Solid gold cannot purchase her,
nor can her price be paid with
silver.
¹⁶She cannot be bought with gold of
Ophir,
with precious onyx or lapis lazuli,
¹⁷Gold or crystal cannot equal her,
nor can golden vessels be ex-
changed for her.

¹⁸Neither coral nor crystal should
be thought of;
the value of wisdom surpasses
pearls.
¹⁹Ethiopian topaz does not equal
her,
nor can she be weighed out for
pure gold.
²⁰As for wisdom, where does she
come from?
Where is the place of understanding?
²¹She is hidden from the eyes of
every living thing;

renewal of traditional wisdom embraced by the book's prologue where "the fear of the Lord is wisdom" (28:28; cf. 1:1, 8; 2:3). For these and other reasons a great number of scholars think this passage is a late addition to the book, added by a subsequent reader to make the debate between Job and his friends more orthodox. That may be so, but in its present place in the book, the chapter serves as a theological comment on the book itself, voiced by its principal character Job. It is as if he has temporarily stepped aside from the debate to comment on it.

In places the Hebrew is obscure. Though some literary sense can be made of the chapter in its original state, this interpretation will follow the NABRE arrangement. The Old Testament personifies Wisdom as a woman (Prov 1:20-33; 3:13-18; 4:5-9; 8:1–9:6), and because the noun "wisdom" is a feminine form in Hebrew, references to Wisdom herself may be present here. She is a controversial figure present at creation and witness to God's creative works (Prov 8:22-36). God acquires her, delights in her, and she, in turn, becomes the bridge between God, creation, and human beings. Some think Wisdom is another way to speak of God, but minimally, at least, she is closely connected to God.

Job begins with an impersonal set of observations about the human endeavor of mining for precious minerals (28:1-6). He observes that humans are able to draw silver and gold, iron and copper, even sapphires from the earth. The earth itself is a vast mystery, for though it produces bread, great fires burn within (28:5). Amazing as is the human capacity to extract things from the ground, the deeper puzzle resides elsewhere and is the theme of the poem. As for wisdom—where can she be found? Where is the place of understanding?" (28:12, and rephrased slightly, 28:20).

even from the birds of the air
she is concealed.
²²Abaddon and Death say,
"Only by rumor have we heard
of her."
²³But God understands the way to
her;
it is he who knows her place.
²⁴For he beholds the ends of the
earth
and sees all that is under the
heavens.

²⁵When he weighed out the wind,
and measured out the waters;
²⁶When he made a rule for the rain
and a path for the thunderbolts,
²⁷Then he saw wisdom and
appraised her,
established her, and searched
her out.
²⁸And to mortals he said:
See: the fear of the Lord is
wisdom;
and avoiding evil is understanding.

Yearning for wisdom centers the poem, as if Job imagines that it is located in a physical spot. He knows that for humans nothing is as precious as wisdom; neither gold nor silver can match its importance (28:13-18). As the sages traditionally hold (Prov 3:14-15; 8:10-11, 19; 16:16), even the most treasured jewels pale compared to the value of wisdom. This observation leads back to the question of verses 12 and 20. Wisdom cannot be found. It is hidden from beasts, birds, and even birds of prey, who sail above the earth and excel at finding food. Nature cannot find it. Both the unfathomable abyss and the sea, here given voices, acknowledge they do not have wisdom. Death and Abbadon, the mythic place of the dead, have only heard rumors about it. The cosmos itself is ignorant of the way to wisdom.

The climax of this hymn is that only God knows the way to her and knows her place (28:23-28). This conclusion surprises because Job has been accusing God of misrule, injustice, and disdain for Job himself, and thus, lack of wisdom. Now in a surprising turn, he identifies the Creator as one who sees the earth, maintains it, splits rocks, fixes boundaries of the waters, and, then, seeing wisdom, becomes one with her. Even more surprising, Job quotes God instructing humans in behavior Job already does: he fears God and avoids evil (28:28; cf. 1:1, 8; 2:3).

Job's hymn comments on the speeches thus far in the book. The debate has not yielded wisdom, though readers know that Job lives a wise life because of his righteous behavior. The chapter also anticipates the speeches in the storm where God appears again as Creator whose wisdom transcends human capacities to grasp. Finally, the poem serves as a tranquil interlude, a space for reconsideration, and an invitation to readers to ask where wisdom resides in this book and in the world.

VI. Job's Final Summary
of His Cause

29 ¹Job took up his theme again and said:

²Oh, that I were as in the months
past,
as in the days when God
watched over me:
³While he kept his lamp shining
above my head,
and by his light I walked
through darkness;
⁴As I was in my flourishing days,
when God sheltered my tent;
⁵When the Almighty was still with
me,
and my children were round
about me;
⁶When my footsteps were bathed in
cream,

and the rock flowed with
streams of oil.
⁷Whenever I went out to the gate of
the city
and took my seat in the square,
⁸The young men saw me and with-
drew,
and the elders rose up and
stood;
⁹Officials refrained from speaking
and covered their mouths with
their hands;
¹⁰The voice of the princes was
silenced,
and their tongues stuck to the
roofs of their mouths.
¹¹The ear that heard blessed me;
the eye that saw acclaimed me.
¹²For I rescued the poor who cried
out for help,
the orphans, and the unassisted⸴

29:1–31:37 Job's final defense

These three chapters form another subunit within Job's long speech (chs. 27–31). They begin with a new introduction (29:1) and proceed as if the hymn to wisdom had never been spoken. Chapter 29 presents the good old days of Job's relationship with God. As if in a divorce court, he sets out the beauty of their former friendship. In the next chapter, he laments the humiliation and loss that characterizes his present life (ch. 30). In chapter 31, he utters a series of solemn oaths to declare his incontestable innocence in very specific terms. His self-defense concludes his words with poignant wishes that someone would hear his case and the Almighty would answer him.

29:1-25 Nostalgia for the past

Job's description of the past is filled with lyric beauty. Nostalgically, he wishes he were back in the times when God watched over him and shed light upon him even as he walked through darkness. In those days God watched over his tent and Job flourished. Interpreting life in a way that echoes the Satan's view (1:9-10), Job claims his familial and material blessings as signs that "the Almighty was still with me" (29:5). He speaks of his "footsteps," that is, all his endeavors, in language of wellbeing and fertility, "bathed in cream" and sustained by "streams of oil" (29:6).

¹³The blessing of those in extremity
came upon me,
and the heart of the widow I
made joyful.
¹⁴I wore my righteousness like a
garment;
justice was my robe and my
turban.
¹⁵I was eyes to the blind,
and feet to the lame was I.
¹⁶I was a father to the poor;
the complaint of the stranger I
pursued,
¹⁷And I broke the jaws of the
wicked man;
from his teeth I forced the prey.
¹⁸I said: "In my own nest I shall
grow old;
I shall multiply years like the
phoenix.
¹⁹My root is spread out to the
waters;

the dew rests by night on my
branches.
²⁰My glory is fresh within me,
and my bow is renewed in my
hand!"
²¹For me they listened and waited;
they were silent for my counsel.
²²Once I spoke, they said no more,
but received my pronouncement
drop by drop.
²³They waited for me as for the rain;
they drank in my words like the
spring rains.
²⁴When I smiled on them they could
not believe it;
they would not let the light of
my face be dimmed.
²⁵I decided their course and sat at
their head,
I lived like a king among the
troops,
like one who comforts mourners.

During that idyllic past, God's blessings extended to Job's social relationships. In a culture of honor and shame, he was a most honored man. When he recalls the way young people and elders, chiefs and princes showed him respect, he is not bragging in an arrogant fashion (29:7-25). Instead, he is remembering evidence of divine blessing upon his life. In contrast to the behavior of his three friends, his community was deferential, gave him proper space, listened to his every word, and waited for him as if they were anticipating the needed rains in spring. Not only was Job personally blessed and honored, he blessed others by his compassionate concern for them. He reassured, comforted, and led them.

Eliphaz had accused him of injustice, of failing to live according to torah, and of refusing to maintain solidarity with the poor (29:11-17). Job argues to the contrary. He rescued the poor, the widow, and the orphan. He lived honestly and justly and helped the disabled like a father to the needy. He fought evil rather than performed it. Because he lived a righteous life and had so many blessings, he expected his good life to continue into his old age. The beauty and power of Job's past was strong and his inner life was rich, for his glory was "fresh within" him and his bow was renewed in his hand (29:20).

30 ¹But now they hold me in derision
who are younger than I,
Whose fathers I should have
disdained
to rank with the dogs of my flock.
²Such strength as they had meant
nothing to me;
their vigor had perished.
³In want and emaciating hunger
they fled to the parched lands:
to the desolate wasteland by
night.
⁴They plucked saltwort and shrubs;
the roots of the broom plant
were their food.
⁵They were banished from the
community,
with an outcry like that against
a thief—
⁶To dwell on the slopes of the
wadies,
in caves of sand and stone;
⁷Among the bushes they brayed;

under the nettles they huddled
together.
⁸Irresponsible, of no account,
they were driven out of the land.
⁹Yet now they sing of me in
mockery;
I have become a byword among
them.
¹⁰They abhor me, they stand aloof,
they do not hesitate to spit in
my face!
¹¹Because he has loosened my bow-
string and afflicted me,
they have thrown off restraint in
my presence.
¹²On my right the young rabble rise
up;
they trip my feet,
they build their approaches for
my ruin.
¹³They tear up my path,
they promote my ruin,
no helper is there against them.

30:1-31 The miserable present

Grief and mourning quickly replace the beauty and joy of Job's past in this lamenting speech. His depiction of the present stands in sharp contrast to the golden past of the previous chapter. Instead of honor, his community now holds him in derision (30:1-15). In this hierarchical society, people who themselves are dishonorable treat Job as lower than they. Young men whose fathers would rank with dogs, who suffer want and hunger and scavenge for food, irresponsible men without names of honor are among his deriders (30:1-8). They mock him and scorn him and lord it over him recklessly (30:11). As they approach him like an army advancing through the breach, terror overtakes him and all seems lost (30:12-15).

Job replaces the plural of the enemies with the singular "he pierces my bones . . . he has cast me into the mire" (30:17-19). God has become his "tormentor" (30:21). The object of Job's complaint switches from his human enemies to the divine enemy who has cast him off. It is the failure of Job's relationship that has destroyed his life and propelled him into his present. The "mire" is a metaphoric description of his suffering that also alludes to Job's place on the ash heap (2:8) and anticipates his response to God in the storm (42:6).

¹⁴As through a wide breach they
     advance;
  amid the uproar they come on
     in waves;
     ¹⁵terrors roll over me.
My dignity is driven off like the
     wind,
  and my well-being vanishes like
     a cloud.
¹⁶And now my life ebbs away from
     me,
  days of affliction have taken
     hold of me.
¹⁷At night he pierces my bones,
  my sinews have no rest.
¹⁸With great difficulty I change my
     clothes,
  the collar of my tunic fits
     around my waist.
¹⁹He has cast me into the mire;
  I have become like dust and
     ashes.
²⁰I cry to you, but you do not
     answer me;
  I stand, but you take no notice.
²¹You have turned into my
     tormentor,
  and with your strong hand you
     attack me.
²²You raise me up and drive me
     before the wind;
  I am tossed about by the tempest.

²³Indeed I know that you will
     return me to death
  to the house destined for every-
     one alive.
²⁴Yet should not a hand be held out
  to help a wretched person in
     distress?
²⁵Did I not weep for the hardships
     of others;
  was not my soul grieved for the
     poor?
²⁶Yet when I looked for good, evil
     came;
  when I expected light, darkness
     came.
²⁷My inward parts seethe and will
     not be stilled;
  days of affliction have overtaken
     me.
²⁸I go about in gloom, without the
     sun;
  I rise in the assembly and cry for
     help.
²⁹I have become a brother to jackals,
  a companion to ostriches.
³⁰My blackened skin falls away
     from me;
  my very frame is scorched by
     the heat.
³¹My lyre is tuned to mourning,
  and my reed pipe to sounds of
     weeping.

Job then speaks directly to God, continuing the divorce proceedings (30:20-25). Their relationship is utterly broken. When Job cries to God there is only silence and mute staring back. He charges God with abuse as God's strong hand strikes him and casts him off into the tempest (30:21-22). God is sending him to death, "the house destined for everyone alive" (30:23). Yet Job appeals again. Should he not receive a helping hand in this calamity, particularly since he had shown compassion and care for the hardships of others?

From his indirect appeal to God, he returns in grief to his own relentless experiences of gloom and hopelessness, as if he knows help will not come (30:26-31). His suffering is constant and its effects are physical (30:17, 30), spiritual (30:16), and psychological (30:26, 28). His only companions are

31 ¹I made a covenant with my eyes
not to gaze upon a virgin.
²What portion comes from God
above,
what heritage from the
Almighty on high?
³Is it not calamity for the
unrighteous,
and woe for evildoers?
⁴Does he not see my ways,
and number all my steps?
⁵If I have walked in falsehood
and my foot has hastened to
deceit,
⁶Let God weigh me in the scales of
justice;
thus will he know my innocence!

⁷If my steps have turned out of the
way,
and my heart has followed my
eyes,
or any stain clings to my hands,
⁸Then may I sow, but another eat,
and may my produce be rooted
up!
⁹If my heart has been enticed
toward a woman,
and I have lain in wait at my
neighbor's door;
¹⁰Then may my wife grind for
another,
and may others kneel over her!
¹¹For that would be heinous,
a crime to be condemned,

---

jackals and ostriches, creatures with whom he shares experiences of human hatred. He mourns the fate of his body and imagines his whole being as a musical instrument of weeping (30:31).

31:1-40 Job's solemn oaths

Perhaps because he has mourned, complained, and expressed his fidelity and innocence, perhaps because he has spoken back to both God and his friends, Job has grown strong and courageous in his sorrows. His expressive words have expanded even as his friends' words have disappeared. Again, Job calls on God to give him a hearing and court and for God to answer his charges (see 13:13-19 and 23:2-7). In this final chapter of his speech, he sets out the case for his innocence in legal terms. He speaks in solemn oaths.

An oath follows the form, "If I have done X, then let Y happen to me" (see Ps 7:4-6). In an oral culture like ancient Israel, words alone guaranteed the reliability of business transactions and legal dealings; hence, their validity was essential to communal life. By uttering oaths, people gave solemnity to their statements, calling curses upon themselves if they were lying. Job uses oaths to force God to declare him guilty or innocent. If Job is guilty, God will execute the curses, but if God keeps silent, then Job will be publicly vindicated. The catalogue of sins Job offers to vindicate himself presents a highly moral picture, for Job declares all his relationships to be honorable and just. To modern readers, Job may appear as a privileged male presiding over women and servants as their superior, but Job is righteous in the terms of his own culture.

71

"I have become a companion to ostriches" (Job 30:29). Job's friends are like the ostriches that bury their heads in the sand of their denial of Job's innocence. Ostriches may also be another example of God's wild and free creatures who are symbols of Job himself.

¹²A fire that would consume down
to Abaddon
till it uprooted all my crops.
¹³Had I refused justice to my man-
servant
or to my maidservant, when
they had a complaint
against me,
¹⁴What then should I do when God
rises up?
What could I answer when he
demands an account?
¹⁵Did not he who made me in the
belly make him?
Did not the same One fashion us
in the womb?
¹⁶If I have denied anything that the
poor desired,
or allowed the eyes of the
widow to languish
¹⁷While I ate my portion alone,
with no share in it for the
fatherless,
¹⁸Though like a father he has reared
me from my youth,
guiding me even from my
mother's womb—
¹⁹If I have seen a wanderer without
clothing,
or a poor man without covering,
²⁰Whose limbs have not blessed me

when warmed with the fleece of
my sheep;
²¹If I have raised my hand against
the innocent
because I saw that I had sup-
porters at the gate—
²²Then may my arm fall from the
shoulder,
my forearm be broken at the
elbow!
²³For I dread calamity from God,
and his majesty will overpower
me.
²⁴Had I put my trust in gold
or called fine gold my security;
²⁵Or had I rejoiced that my wealth
was great,
or that my hand had acquired
abundance—
²⁶Had I looked upon the light as it
shone,
or the moon in the splendor of
its progress,
²⁷And had my heart been secretly
enticed
to blow them a kiss with my
hand,
²⁸This too would be a crime for
condemnation,
for I should have denied God
above.

With sixteen oaths, Job catalogues sins of which he declares himself innocent. The chapter begins with general claims about God's legacy to humans, a legacy that appears to contradict Job's own experience (31:2-6). He asks if calamity befalls the unrighteous. His next question directly charges God with failure to see. He knows if God weighs him in the scales of justice, he will be shown to be innocent.

Job begins his oath with a central virtue of communal life, honesty (31:5-7). He has not lied, deceived, or stained his hands with bribery or thievery, or any kind of offense. If he has, then he will plant like a laborer, but his neighbor will reap the rewards.

The next cluster of oaths concerns Job's life of social justice (31:13-23). He has treated fairly all claims of his servants against him, and he acknowledges

²⁹Had I rejoiced at the destruction
of my enemy
or exulted when evil came upon
him,
³⁰Even though I had not allowed
my mouth to sin
by invoking a curse against his
life—
³¹Had not the men of my tent
exclaimed,
"Who has not been filled with
his meat!"
³²No stranger lodged in the street,
for I opened my door to
wayfarers—
³³Had I, all too human, hidden my
sins
and buried my guilt in my bosom
³⁴Because I feared the great
multitude

and the scorn of the clans
terrified me—
then I should have remained
silent, and not come out
of doors!
³⁵Oh, that I had one to hear my case:
here is my signature: let the
Almighty answer me!
Let my accuser write out his
indictment!
³⁶Surely, I should wear it on my
shoulder
or put it on me like a diadem;
³⁷Of all my steps I should give him
an account;
like a prince I should present
myself before him.
³⁸If my land has cried out against
me
till its furrows wept together;

---

the common humanity they share (31:15). He has never denied the poor, the widow, or the orphan, the naked or the hungry, nor has he harmed the innocent in league with other important men at the city gates. If he has, then his own arm will be severed from his body and God will overpower him (31:22).

If he has abused the land (31:38-40), then the land will retaliate by producing weeds instead of food (31:1, 9-12). If he has even been tempted by a woman or stalked her, then may his wife become a sexual slave to others. Because women were second-class citizens in much of the ancient world, assaults on one's wife were a dishonor to their husbands who could not protect them.

The theological side of injustice is idolatry (31:24-28). Job neither worshiped gold nor gloated over his wealth, nor did he deny God by worshiping the sun and moon as did some in ancient Israel (2 Kgs 21:3ff; Deut 4:19; Jer 8:2; Ezek 8:16). He treated his enemies well and extended hospitality toward the stranger, as required not only by custom in the ancient world but also by Hebrew law. Nor was Job self-righteous and hypocritical, never hiding his sins to save his reputation (31:33-34).

Job's oaths make clear that he believes himself innocent of moral transgression in all phases of his life. If he has committed sins to deserve his suffering, he is unaware of it. As readers have known from the beginning, he is a blameless and upright man who fears God and avoids evil (1:1),

³⁹If I have eaten its strength without
payment
and grieved the hearts of its
tenants;
⁴⁰Then let the thorns grow instead
of wheat
and stinkweed instead of barley!
The words of Job are ended.

VII. Elihu's Speeches

32 ¹Then the three men ceased to answer Job, because in his own eyes he was in the right. ²But the anger of Elihu, son of Barachel the Buzite, of the clan of Ram, was kindled. He was angry with Job for considering himself rather

---

but no one else among his community knows this. He does not deserve his suffering as his friends maintain, and God has abandoned him.

Job concludes his words with a final wish for someone to hear his case (31:35-37). Perhaps, like his earlier desire to have a mediator bring him and God together in a courtroom (9:33), he wants his adversary to write out an indictment. This would make the charges public and, above all, evident to him. Or perhaps the document would be a writ of exoneration, since Job has declared his innocence. Either way, Job would be so liberated and empowered by this document that he would wear it before the public and present himself like a prince. He concludes with a challenge for the Almighty to answer him (31:37).

Job began his speeches in chapter 3 with a desire for death to come and for his life and its beginnings to be obliterated from creation. He ends his words, having lamented his many sorrows, raged at God, despaired of his friends, and protested with full force the theology of which he had been a former proponent. No longer does that theology stand. The wicked are not punished and the innocent are not protected from the horrors of this world. One does not always and inevitably reap what one has sown.

Job protests this theology and in the process begins to undergo transformation. His rage at God emerges not as blasphemy but as an expression of his fidelity. Throughout his long, dark night he has clung to God, even if in biting critique of God's management of the world. He shouts at God, disparages God, but he never abandons God, even though he believes God has abandoned him.

Readers now expect God to step forward and reply to Job, but, instead, a fourth friend named Elihu comes onto the stage.

ELIHU SPEAKS

Job 32:1–37:24

Elihu appears suddenly in the book of Job. He has not been mentioned before, nor counted among the three friends who comfort Job on the ash

than God to be in the right. ³He was angry also with the three friends because they had not found a good answer and had not condemned Job. ⁴But since these men were older than he, Elihu bided his time before addressing Job. ⁵When, however, Elihu saw that there was no reply in the mouths of the three men, his wrath was inflamed. ⁶So Elihu, son of Barachel the Buzite, answered and said:

I am young and you are very old;
therefore I held back and was
afraid
to declare to you my knowledge.
⁷I thought, days should speak,
and many years teach wisdom!
⁸But there is a spirit in human
beings,
the breath of the Almighty, that
gives them understanding.

⁹It is not those of many days who
are wise,
nor the aged who understand
the right.
¹⁰Therefore I say, listen to me;
I also will declare my knowledge!
¹¹Behold, I have waited for your
words,
have given ear to your
arguments,
as you searched out what to say.
¹²Yes, I followed you attentively:
And look, none of you has
convicted Job,
not one could refute his
statements.
¹³So do not say, "We have met
wisdom;
God can vanquish him but no
mortal!"
¹⁴For had he addressed his words to
me,

---

heap, and he completely disappears after his speeches. For a number of reasons, including his abrupt appearance, many interpreters think Elihu's speeches are a later addition to the book, perhaps by a writer who wanted to make the book more orthodox. Elihu both repeats some of the claims of the friends and anticipates some of God's speech in the whirlwind, making his words seem unnecessary. But from a literary point of view, Elihu's speech creates a dramatic delay and builds tension before God appears in the storm. Moreover, Elihu asserts that humans cannot discover God, so God's appearance becomes more striking and unexpected.

By introducing Elihu (32:1-5) and repeatedly announcing across the chapters that he is continuing to speak (34:1; 35:1; 36:1), a narrator divides Elihu's speeches into four parts (32:6–33:33; 34:1-37; 35:1-16; 36:1–37:24). These announcements of continuation may indicate the work of an editor who incorporated pre-existing material into the book or, more likely, they may highlight one of Elihu's character flaws. He is long-winded.

32:1-5 Introduction

Though debated among interpreters, the introduction offers clues to what follows. This is the first significant intrusion of a narrator since the prose prologue (chs. 1–2). The narrator introduces Elihu as an angry man

I would not then have answered
    him with your words.
15They are dismayed, they make no
    more reply;
    words fail them.
16Must I wait? Now that they speak
    no more,
    and have ceased to make reply,
17I too will speak my part;
    I also will declare my knowledge!
18For I am full of words;
    the spirit within me compels
    me.
19My belly is like unopened wine,
    like wineskins ready to burst.
20Let me speak and obtain relief;
    let me open my lips, and reply.
21I would not be partial to anyone,
    nor give flattering titles to any.
22For I know nothing of flattery;
    if I did, my Maker would soon
    take me away.

33 1Therefore, O Job, hear my
    discourse;
    listen to all my words.

2Behold, now I open my mouth;
    my tongue and voice form
    words.
3I will state directly what is in my
    mind,
    my lips shall speak knowledge
    clearly;
4For the spirit of God made me,
    the breath of the Almighty
    keeps me alive.
5If you are able, refute me;
    draw up your arguments and
    take your stand.
6Look, I am like you before God,
    I too was pinched from clay.
7Therefore fear of me should not
    dismay you,
    nor should I weigh heavily
    upon you.
8But you have said in my hearing,
    as I listened to the sound of
    your words:
9"I am clean, without transgression;
    I am innocent, there is no guilt
    in me.

(32:2). Next he presents Elihu's family tree, an honor provided for no other character in the book. It is possible that the Hebrew names of Elihu's ancestry mock him by referring to a contemptuous one who is high and mighty. The narrator expands Elihu's motivation for speaking. He is angry because the friends failed either to answer or to condemn Job. He waited to speak only because he was showing respect to his elders. Then for the fourth time, we learn about his wrath; it was "inflamed" (32:5). Elihu's words are passionate, but they are not necessarily judicious.

32:6–33:33 Elihu's first speech

Elihu introduces himself as a youth, and then chides his elders for not speaking words of wisdom. He spends the entire first chapter introducing himself and telling why he must speak. In the process, he confirms the narrator's suggestions about his character. The three friends are not inspired by the Almighty because the spirit, not experience, gives understanding. He commands everyone to listen to him, implying that he alone has received the spirit. He accuses the friends of failing to refute Job (32:12-14). He even

¹⁰Yet he invents pretexts against me
and counts me as an enemy.
¹¹He puts my feet in the stocks,
watches all my paths!"
¹²In this you are not just, let me tell
you;
for God is greater than mortals.
¹³Why, then, do you make
complaint against him
that he gives no reply to their
words?
¹⁴For God does speak, once,
even twice, though you do not
see it:
¹⁵In a dream, in a vision of the night,
when deep sleep falls upon
mortals
as they slumber in their beds.
¹⁶It is then he opens their ears
and with a warning, terrifies
them,
¹⁷By turning mortals from acting
and keeping pride away from a
man,

¹⁸He holds his soul from the pit,
his life from passing to the
grave.
¹⁹Or he is chastened on a bed of
pain,
suffering continually in his
bones,
²⁰So that to his appetite food is
repulsive,
his throat rejects the choicest
nourishment.
²¹His flesh is wasted, it cannot be
seen;
bones, once invisible, appear;
²²His soul draws near to the pit,
his life to the place of the dead.
²³If then there be a divine messenger, ▷
a mediator, one out of a
thousand,
to show him what is right,
²⁴He will take pity on him and say,
"Deliver him from going down
to the pit;
I have found him a ransom."

admits he is full of words given by the spirit and is ready to burst (32:18-19). That he does not know how to flatter is evident already to readers (32:22).

In the next chapter (33:1-33), Elihu appeals directly to Job and demands that he listen. Offering some comic relief in this otherwise somber book, he continues to announce that he is going to speak, that the spirit of God inspired him to speak, and that Job should prepare to rebut him without fear of him (33:2-7). Finally, he gets to his point in a direct manner. He claims to quote Job in order to argue against him. His quotes, however, convey the sense of Job's words but not his direct speech (33:9-11). Elihu tells Job he is unjust to God. Because God is greater than humans, Job has no place in demanding an account. When God does speak, one may not even know it. When God warns with terrors of the night or sends illness and suffering, it is to save the person from death (33:14-22).

Like Job, Elihu also hopes for a mediator between God and humans, not to control God as Job had hoped (9:32-35), or to witness on Job's behalf (16:19), but to bring Job around and save him. Elihu and Job have opposite opinions as to the role of the heavenly mediator. The effects of the mediator's guidance will be to restore Job to singing and rejoicing as God restores

²⁵Then his flesh shall become soft as
a boy's;
he shall be again as in the days
of his youth.
²⁶He shall pray and God will favor
him;
he shall see God's face with
rejoicing;
for he restores a person's
righteousness.
²⁷He shall sing before all and say,
"I sinned and did wrong,
yet I was not punished
accordingly.
²⁸He delivered me from passing to
the pit,
and my life sees light."
²⁹See, all these things God does,
two, even three times, for a man,
³⁰Bringing back his soul from the pit
to the light, in the light of the
living.
³¹Be attentive, Job, listen to me!
Be silent and I will speak.
³²If you have anything to say, then
answer me.
Speak out! I should like to see
you justified.
³³If not, then you listen to me;
be silent, and I will teach you
wisdom.

34 ¹Then Elihu answered and said:
²Hear my discourse, you that
are wise;
you that have knowledge, listen
to me!

³For the ear tests words,
as the palate tastes food.
⁴Let us choose what is right;
let us determine among
ourselves what is good.
⁵For Job has said, "I am innocent,
but God has taken away what is
my right.
⁶I declare the judgment on me to be
a lie;
my arrow-wound is incurable,
sinless though I am."
⁷What man is like Job?
He drinks in blasphemies like
water,
⁸Keeps company with evildoers
and goes along with the wicked,
⁹When he says, "There is no profit
in pleasing God."
¹⁰Therefore, you that have
understanding, hear me:
far be it from God to do
wickedness;
far from the Almighty to do
wrong!
¹¹Rather, he requites mortals for
their conduct,
and brings home to them their
way of life.
¹²Surely, God cannot act wickedly,
the Almighty cannot pervert
justice.
¹³Who gave him charge over the
earth,
or who set all the world in its
place?

---

his soul from the realm of death (33:25-30). In an arrogant manner, Elihu urges Job to listen silently, unless he has something to say. As a younger man speaking to an elder in a culture that honors the elder, he is quite overbearing. Perhaps he thinks he is Job's mediator.

34:1-37 Elihu's second speech

Elihu treats Job's three friends with the same disrespect he shows Job, addressing them as wise men while he mocks their wisdom. He invites

¹⁴If he were to set his mind to it,
    gather to himself his spirit and
        breath,
¹⁵All flesh would perish together,
    and mortals return to dust.
¹⁶Now you—understand, hear this!
    Listen to the words I speak!
¹⁷Can an enemy of justice be in
        control,
    will you condemn the supreme
        Just One,
¹⁸Who says to a king, "You are
        worthless!"
    and to nobles, "You are wicked!"
¹⁹Who neither favors the person of
        princes,
    nor respects the rich more than
        the poor?
For they are all the work of his
    hands;
        ²⁰in a moment they die, even at
            midnight.
People are shaken, and pass away,
    the powerful are removed
        without lifting a hand;
²¹For his eyes are upon our ways,
    and all our steps he sees.
²²There is no darkness so dense
    that evildoers can hide in it.
²³For no one has God set a time
    to come before him in judgment.
²⁴Without inquiry he shatters the
        mighty,
    and appoints others in their
        place,
²⁵Thus he discerns their works;

overnight they are crushed.
²⁶Where the wicked are, he strikes
        them,
    in a place where all can see,
²⁷Because they turned away from
        him
    and did not understand his
        ways at all:
²⁸And made the cry of the poor
        reach him,
    so that he heard the cry of the
        afflicted.
²⁹If he is silent, who then can
        condemn?
    If he hides his face, who then
        can behold him,
    whether nation or individual?
³⁰Let an impious man not rule,
    nor those who ensnare their
        people.
³¹Should anyone say to God,
    "I accept my punishment; I will
        offend no more;
³²What I cannot see, teach me:
    if I have done wrong, I will do
        so no more,"
³³Would you then say that God
        must punish,
    when you are disdainful?
It is you who must choose, not I;
    speak, therefore, what you
        know.
³⁴Those who understand will say to
        me,
    all the wise who hear my views:
³⁵"Job speaks without knowledge,

---

them to discern the truth with him, though he has already decided what it is. Again he quotes Job to discredit his speech, interpreting his words and his person as evil. With even more arrogance, he instructs the friends about God's justice in traditional terms (34:10-15). God does not respect humans for wealth or power but focuses on their ways and dispenses justice with inescapable speed. He condemns Job further by assuming that the wise will agree with him in dismissing Job's claim to wisdom. He deserves punishment because his rebellious words compound his sins.

his words make no sense.
³⁶Let Job be tested to the limit,
　　since his answers are those of
　　　the impious;
³⁷For he is adding rebellion to his sin
　　by brushing off our arguments
　　and addressing many words to
　　　God."

35 ¹Then Elihu answered and said:
²Do you think it right to say,
　　"I am in the right, not God"?
³When you ask what it profits you,
　　"What advantage do I have
　　　from not sinning?"
⁴I have words for a reply to you
　　and your friends as well.
⁵Look up to the skies and see;
　　behold the heavens high above
　　　you.
⁶If you sin, what do you do to God?
　　Even if your offenses are many,
　　　how do you affect him?
⁷If you are righteous, what do you
　　give him,
　　or what does he receive from
　　　your hand?
⁸Your wickedness affects only
　　someone like yourself,
　　and your justice, only a fellow
　　　human being.
⁹In great oppression people cry out;
　　they call for help because of the
　　　power of the great,

¹⁰No one says, "Where is God, my
　　Maker,
　　who gives songs in the night,
¹¹Teaches us more than the beasts of
　　the earth,
　　and makes us wiser than the
　　　birds of the heavens?"
¹²Though thus they cry out, he does
　　not answer
　　because of the pride of the
　　　wicked.
¹³But it is idle to say God does not
　　hear
　　or that the Almighty does not
　　　take notice.
¹⁴Even though you say, "You take
　　no notice of it,"
　　the case is before him; with
　　　trembling wait upon him.
¹⁵But now that you have done
　　otherwise, God's anger
　　　punishes,
　　nor does he show much concern
　　　over a life.
¹⁶Yet Job to no purpose opens his
　　mouth,
　　multiplying words without
　　　knowledge.

36 ¹Elihu continued and said:
²Wait a little and I will instruct
　　you,
　　for there are still words to be
　　　said for God.

35:1-6 Elihu's third speech

Elihu continues interrogating Job. Why does Job think it proper to claim he is just and God is not? (35:1-3). He wants Job to recognize and submit to the transcendence of God beyond all things human (35:4-12). No human behavior can affect God, even that of the oppressed who cry out. God does not respond to human cries. The Hebrew of the next verses is not entirely clear, but Elihu maintains that Job's words are meaningless (35:16).

36:1–37:24 Elihu's fourth speech

Elihu keeps his windbag character by telling us again that he is going to speak to illuminate Job's situation (36:2-4). When he finally gets to the

³I will assemble arguments from
afar,
and for my maker I will establish what is right.
⁴For indeed, my words are not a lie;
one perfect in knowledge is before you.
⁵Look, God is great, not disdainful;
his strength of purpose is great.
He does not preserve the life of the
wicked.
⁶He establishes the right of the
poor;
he does not divert his eyes from
the just
⁷But he seats them upon thrones
with kings, exalted forever.
⁸If they are bound with fetters,
held fast by bonds of affliction,
⁹He lets them know what they have
done,
and how arrogant are their sins.
¹⁰He opens their ears to correction
and tells them to turn back from
evil.
¹¹If they listen and serve him,
they spend their days in
prosperity,
their years in happiness.

¹²But if they do not listen, they pass
to the grave,
they perish for lack of
knowledge.
¹³The impious in heart lay up anger;
they do not cry for help when
he binds them;
¹⁴They will die young—
their life among the reprobate.
¹⁵But he saves the afflicted through
their affliction,
and opens their ears through
oppression.
¹⁶He entices you from distress,
to a broad place without
constraint;
what rests on your table is rich
food.
¹⁷Though you are full of the judgment of the wicked,
judgment and justice will be
maintained.
¹⁸Let not anger at abundance entice
you,
nor great bribery lead you
astray.
¹⁹Will your wealth equip you
against distress,
or all your exertions of strength?

knowledge he brings "from afar" (36:3), it amounts to reiteration of arguments already given by the friends that God rewards the good and punishes
the wicked (36:4-21). Though God is not affected by any human behavior
according to the previous chapter, God does respond to human behavior
by punishing the wicked. God reveals sins to correct the disobedient and
causes the disobedient to perish. Suffering and distress are educational for
some and God sends affliction to save them (36:15). Verses 16-21 are nearly
unreadable in the Hebrew.

Much of the remainder of Elihu's speech anticipates the words of God
in the storm (36:22–37:22). His theme is the power and wonder of creation.
He advises Job to consider that God is transcendent, beyond human connection, as revealed in God's providential control of the cosmos (36:22-25).
In the ancient world, the workings of sun and rain, of stars and seasons,
were profound mysteries. Elihu finds a nearly sacramental sense in the

²⁰Do not long for the night,
  when peoples vanish in their
    place.
²¹Be careful; do not turn to evil;
  for this you have preferred to
    affliction.
²²Look, God is exalted in his power.
  What teacher is there like him?
²³Who prescribes for him his way?
  Who says, "You have done
    wrong"?
²⁴Remember, you should extol his
    work,
  which people have praised in
    song.
²⁵All humankind beholds it;
  everyone views it from afar.
²⁶See, God is great beyond our
    knowledge,
  the number of his years past
    searching out.
²⁷He holds in check the waterdrops
  that filter in rain from his flood,
²⁸Till the clouds flow with them
  and they rain down on all hu-
    mankind.
²⁹Can anyone understand the
    spreading clouds,
  the thunderings from his tent?
³⁰Look, he spreads his light over it,
  it covers the roots of the sea.
³¹For by these he judges the nations,
  and gives food in abundance.
³²In his hands he holds the lightning,

and he commands it to strike
    the mark.
³³His thunder announces him
  and incites the fury of the storm.

37 ¹At this my heart trembles
  and leaps out of its place.
²Listen to his angry voice
  and the rumble that comes forth
    from his mouth!
³Everywhere under the heavens he
    sends it,
  with his light, to the ends of the
    earth.
⁴Again his voice roars,
  his majestic voice thunders;
  he does not restrain them when
    his voice is heard.
⁵God thunders forth marvels with
    his voice;
  he does great things beyond our
    knowing.
⁶He says to the snow, "Fall to the
    earth";
  likewise to his heavy, drenching
    rain.
⁷He shuts up all humankind
    indoors,
  so that all people may know his
    work.
⁸The wild beasts take to cover
  and remain quiet in their dens.
⁹Out of its chamber the tempest
    comes forth;
  from the north winds, the cold.

---

world, an expression of divine life when God uses the rains to nourish nations and provide food (36:26-32). Offering personal testimony, he speaks of storms as God's angry and controlling voice (36:33–37:9). Even hail and frost serve God's purposes (37:10-13).

Elihu commands Job to listen and contemplate God's works. He demands to know if Job understands how God creates light behind clouds, and if Job participates in creating the firmament with God (37:15-18). After six long chapters, he concludes that humans cannot discover the Almighty because God is beyond all accounting. None can see him (37:22-24).

¹⁰With his breath God brings the
    frost,
    and the broad waters congeal.
¹¹The clouds too are laden with
    moisture,
    the storm-cloud scatters its light.
¹²He it is who changes their rounds,
    according to his plans,
    to do all that he commands
    them
    across the inhabited world.
¹³Whether for punishment or mercy,
    he makes it happen.
¹⁴Listen to this, Job!
    Stand and consider the marvels
    of God!
¹⁵Do you know how God lays his
    command upon them,
    and makes the light shine forth
    from his clouds?
¹⁶Do you know how the clouds are
    banked,
    the marvels of him who is per-
    fect in knowledge?
¹⁷You, who swelter in your clothes
    when calm lies over the land
    from the south,
¹⁸Can you with him spread out the
    firmament of the skies,
    hard as a molten mirror?

¹⁹Teach us then what we shall say to
    him;
    we cannot, for the darkness,
    make our plea.
²⁰Will he be told about it when I
    speak?
    Can anyone talk when he is
    being destroyed?
²¹Rather, it is as the light that cannot
    be seen
    while it is obscured by the clouds,
    till the wind comes by and
    sweeps them away.
²²From Zaphon the golden splendor
    comes,
    surrounding God's awesome
    majesty!
²³The Almighty! We cannot find
    him,
    preeminent in power and judg-
    ment,
    abundant in justice, who never
    oppresses.
²⁴Therefore people fear him;
    none can see him, however wise
    their hearts.

VIII. The Lord and Job Meet

38 ¹Then the Lord answered Job out
    of the storm and said:

Surely Elihu is an intruder on the scene, but his speech acts as a thematic bridge between the debates of Job and his friends and the speeches of God still to come. In comic, bombastic terms that violate the customs of the day and disrespect the previous speakers, Elihu builds anticipation and makes Job's three older friends look good by comparison.

THE SPEECHES IN THE STORM

Job 38:1–42:6

Elihu's insistence that "we cannot find" God (37:23) makes God's appearance in the storm all the more dramatic and surprising. Job alone hoped

²Who is this who darkens counsel
    with words of ignorance?
³Gird up your loins now, like a
    man;
    I will question you, and you tell
        me the answers!
⁴Where were you when I founded
    the earth?
    Tell me, if you have under-
        standing.
⁵Who determined its size? Surely
    you know?
    Who stretched out the measuring
        line for it?
⁶Into what were its pedestals sunk,
    and who laid its cornerstone,
⁷While the morning stars sang
    together
    and all the sons of God shouted
        for joy?
⁸Who shut within doors the sea,
    when it burst forth from the
        womb,
⁹When I made the clouds its
    garment

and thick darkness its swaddling
    bands?
¹⁰When I set limits for it
    and fastened the bar of its door,
¹¹And said: Thus far shall you come
    but no farther,
    and here shall your proud
        waves stop?
¹²Have you ever in your lifetime
    commanded the morning
    and shown the dawn its place
¹³For taking hold of the ends of the
    earth,
    till the wicked are shaken from
        it?
¹⁴The earth is changed as clay by
    the seal,
    and dyed like a garment;
¹⁵But from the wicked their light is
    withheld,
    and the arm of pride is shattered.
¹⁶Have you entered into the sources
    of the sea,
    or walked about on the bottom
        of the deep?

---

for such a meeting, but the friends insisted God was inaccessible and did not need to speak because divine justice was already clearly revealed in human life and in the world of animals and plants. In these speeches, as in the prologue, God's name again becomes Yahweh, ("the LORD"), the personal name revealed in Exodus 3. Throughout the long debates between Job and his friends, God was often called by the ancient title, El Shaddai, translated by the NABRE with the traditional "the Almighty." The name Yahweh reveals the God of the storm to be the God of Israel's story, even though the book's characters are foreigners and the book makes no clear reference to historical events.

Although the primary speaker in the storm is the Lord, Job also speaks to create a form of dialogue between them (40:3-5 and 42:1-6). These speeches appear in the book as one more set of arguments in the debate, yet their climactic position and the divine authority of the main speaker grant them significance beyond the others. Carefully structured thematically, they progress through the creation of the cosmos to the wonders of the animal world, and then concentrate on particular animals called Behemoth and Leviathan.

¹⁷Have the gates of death been
    shown to you,
  or have you seen the gates of
    darkness?
¹⁸Have you comprehended the
    breadth of the earth?
  Tell me, if you know it all.
¹⁹What is the way to the dwelling of
    light,
  and darkness—where is its
    place?
²⁰That you may take it to its territory
  and know the paths to its home?
²¹You know, because you were born
    then,
  and the number of your days is
    great!
²²Have you entered the storehouses
    of the snow,
  and seen the storehouses of the
    hail
²³Which I have reserved for times of
    distress,
  for a day of war and battle?
²⁴What is the way to the parting of
    the winds,
  where the east wind spreads
    over the earth?
²⁵Who has laid out a channel for the
  downpour

and a path for the thunderstorm
²⁶To bring rain to uninhabited land,
  the unpeopled wilderness;
²⁷To drench the desolate wasteland
  till the desert blooms with
    verdure?
²⁸Has the rain a father?
  Who has begotten the drops of
    dew?
²⁹Out of whose womb comes the
    ice,
  and who gives the hoarfrost its
    birth in the skies,
³⁰When the waters lie covered as
    though with stone
  that holds captive the surface of
    the deep?
³¹Have you tied cords to the
    Pleiades,
  or loosened the bonds of Orion?
³²Can you bring forth the Mazzaroth
    in their season,
  or guide the Bear with her
    children?
³³Do you know the ordinances of
    the heavens;
  can you put into effect their plan
    on the earth?
³⁴Can you raise your voice to the
    clouds,

38:1–40:2 Creation of the cosmos and its non-human inhabitants
40:3-5   Job's silence
40:6–41:26 Creation of Behemoth and Leviathan
42:1-6   Job's Enigmatic Response

These speeches are as puzzling as they are beautiful. A major interpretive question of the book is how the speeches relate to what precedes and follows them. To this point, the major question of the debate has been why Job suffers, and thus far, no consensus has emerged among the speakers. Readers might, therefore, expect God to settle matters between Job and his friends. Instead, God changes the subject, interrogating Job about his knowledge of creation. Equally puzzling are Job's responses to God's words. In his first response, he silences himself; in the second, he ignores his promise not to speak again, and the words he speaks are ambiguous.

for them to cover you with a
deluge of waters?
[35]Can you send forth the lightnings
on their way,
so that they say to you, "Here
we are"?
[36]Who gives wisdom to the ibis,
and gives the rooster understanding?
[37]Who counts the clouds with
wisdom?
Who tilts the water jars of heaven

[38]So that the dust of earth is fused
into a mass
and its clods stick together?
[39]Do you hunt the prey for the lion
or appease the hunger of young
lions,
[40]While they crouch in their dens,
or lie in ambush in the thicket?
[41]Who provides nourishment for
the raven
when its young cry out to God,
wandering about without food?

Another interpretive issue regarding events in the storm is how to understand God's questioning of Job. Do God's questions disrespect or belittle Job and his suffering? Is God introducing new themes to set Job's suffering in a different perspective? Some scholars think the speeches portray God as a bully who uses superior knowledge and power to silence, shame, and overpower Job. In this view, God appears as the stronger one who out-talks Job the talker, and God disrespects and intimidates Job. But by attending to the poetic imagery of creation, the subject about which Job is ignorant, other interpretations are possible. Rather than doing battle with Job by means of the creation, God celebrates it in its beauty, wildness, and freedom. The speeches portray the breath-stopping creativity of God, the generative beauty of the cosmos and its inhabitants, and the wild freedom of God's creatures. This experience transforms Job.

To grasp the power of these chapters, it is best not to think of God's words as didactic answers to Job's questioning, angry laments. Rather than prosaic instruction, these speeches are lyric poetry, hymn-like speeches, celebrating creation, the amazing web of life in its awesomeness and beauty. They describe what ecologists might call "the household of life," overflowing with energy and freedom. But, of course, readers wonder how these divine speeches relate to Job's suffering?

Together God's speeches form a thematic symmetry between Job's first outburst and events in the storm. Job himself introduced the subject of creation in the curse of his birth (3:1-26). There he tries to "uncreate" the cosmos, to turn day into night, light into darkness, and life into death. God replies to Job's rhetorical destruction of creation with rhetorical reconstruction and recreation. These questions re-establish the world from the bottom up, from the waters, to the stars, to the animal inhabitants.

"Then the Lord answered Job out of the storm" (Job 38:17).

39 ¹Do you know when mountain
goats are born,
or watch for the birth pangs of
deer,
²Number the months that they
must fulfill,
or know when they give birth,
³When they crouch down and drop
their young,
when they deliver their
progeny?

⁴Their offspring thrive and grow in
the open,
they leave and do not return.
⁵Who has given the wild donkey
his freedom,
and who has loosed the wild ass
from bonds?
⁶I have made the wilderness his
home
and the salt flats his dwelling.
⁷He scoffs at the uproar of the city,
hears no shouts of a driver.

The setting of the encounter is a tempest, a whirlwind or fierce storm (38:1). In the Old Testament storms are sometimes the setting for theophanies, that is, appearances of God to humans (Exod 19:16-20; 1 Kgs 19:11-13; Ps 18:7-17; Hab 3:14). Besides being a conventional place of divine-human encounter, the storm conveys divine power and mystery. But the storm also evokes Job's stormy life of suffering, as well as the deaths of his children who lost their lives in a "great wind" (1:19). Job meets God face to face in the stormy chaos of his destroyed world, not in a safe haven protected from harm and tragedy. Finally, if the storm is not only the venue for God's appearance but also an aspect of revelation itself, then the storm implies a deity who is wild, beautiful, free, and deeply unsettling. The speeches do not explain suffering, but they do present Job's anguished sorrows as the place of divine encounter.

38:1–40:2 Yahweh's first speech

The many ambiguities of the divine speech begin in the introductory verses (38:1-3). God interrogates Job like an impatient judge speaking before a courtroom. Annoyance with Job appears to drive the first question. What does God mean by asking "Who is this who darkens counsel with words of ignorance?" God surely knows who Job is, since God previously called him "my servant Job" (1:8; 2:3). Is this question a literary device by which God draws attention to Job's words? Could it be Elihu to whom these words refer? Is this a statement of divine impatience, or is it a testing of the character, as if to ask, "What are you made of Job? Can you stand toe to toe with the Creator of the cosmos?" God then commands Job to prepare for battle by girding his loins. He calls Job by a Hebrew word, translated "man" in the NABRE, that means specifically a "man who is charged as military protector of women and children," that is, one ready for battle. Then God turns the tables to announce that it is now Job's place to be interrogated.

⁸He ranges the mountains for
    pasture,
    and seeks out every patch of
        green.
⁹Will the wild ox consent to serve
    you,
    or pass the nights at your
        manger?
¹⁰Will you bind the wild ox with a
    rope in the furrow,
    and will he plow the valleys
        after you?
¹¹Will you depend on him for his
    great strength
    and leave to him the fruits of
        your toil?
¹²Can you rely on him to bring in
    your grain

and gather in the yield of your
    threshing floor?
¹³The wings of the ostrich flap
    away;
    her plumage is lacking in
        feathers.
¹⁴When she abandons her eggs on
    the ground
    and lets them warm in the sand,
¹⁵She forgets that a foot may crush
    them,
    that the wild beasts may
        trample them;
¹⁶She cruelly disowns her young
    and her labor is useless; she has
        no fear.
¹⁷For God has withheld wisdom
    from her

The subject of the interrogation is Job's knowledge of creation. Asking if Job knows who, where, and when, God picks up the creation theme Job introduced in his curse of his birth where he wanted to unmake God's creation of him (ch. 3). God depicts the cosmos as if it were a habitat, a large building for living creatures. Where was Job when God founded the earth? Does Job know its size, how it rests upon pedestals, or who placed its cornerstone? Was Job a witness when the morning stars sang like a choir? Of course, Job knows nothing about creation, nor can he reach back in memory to the beginnings of the world and the joyous chorus of stars that sang at creation. The ancients believed that the earth itself rested on pedestals and a great dome held the planets and the stars and separated the waters above from the waters below (Gen 1:6).

In a reimagining of the creation story (Gen 1:1–2:4), God asks about Job's knowledge of the sea (38:8-11), conceived as a newborn babe emerging from God's womb, dressed by mother God in swaddling clothes of clouds and darkness, and kept within its limits like a baby in its playpen. From there God speaks of light (38:12-15), asking Job if he has commanded the day to begin and understands how the morning light changes the earth's appearance. Echoing the hymn to Wisdom (ch. 28), verses 16 and 17 attend to the sources of the sea, depths of the abyss, and gates of death.

These verses express ancient understandings of creation, its beginnings, the existence of the underworld, and sources of light, snow, hail, the winds, and the rain (38:22-38). With exquisite beauty, they set forth cosmic imagery

and given her no share in understanding. ¹⁸Yet when she spreads her wings high, she laughs at a horse and rider. ¹⁹Do you give the horse his strength, and clothe his neck with a mane? ²⁰Do you make him quiver like a locust, while his thunderous snorting spreads terror?	²¹He paws the valley, he rejoices in his strength, and charges into battle. ²²He laughs at fear and cannot be terrified; he does not retreat from the sword. ²³Around him rattles the quiver, flashes the spear and the javelin. ²⁴Frenzied and trembling he devours the ground; he does not hold back at the sound of the trumpet;

of birth and nourishment. The heavenly constellations, in their mysterious appearances in each season (38:31-33), challenge Job's understanding of the rules governing heavenly bodies and his command of thunder and lightning. But Job is out of his depth. Only Wisdom was there with God at creation's beginning (Prov 8:22-36). God proudly points to each facet of the cosmos, showing it off to Job like a new homeowner delighting and bragging about her new home.

After God describes the wonders of the cosmic habitat, God interrogates Job about the inscrutable ways of its animal inhabitants (39:1-30). Equally beautiful and filled with the wild life-energy, diverse and unique, these creatures also confound Job. It is possible these animals come from royal lists of hunted animals and the icons that symbolized kings and their power. Some interpreters propose that these animals are negative in their association with wilderness and chaos, but if so, here they come firmly within divine control. Yet God's control of the earth and its animal inhabitants is not a subject of these speeches. Rather God appears to be bragging about the animals who occupy this magnificent habitat in their mysterious ways and stunning freedom. Regardless of the origins of this mixed list of creatures, each of them is beautiful, as well as joyously alive. With God's approval and expressive pride, each acts independently according to its own rhythms.

God's focus with the first three animals concerns the care and sustenance of their young (38:39–39:4). Lions, ravens, and mountain goats feed and give birth to their progeny. Does Job understand the various ways of birth in the animal world, each creature following its own times of gestation? The wild ass, the ox, and ostrich also live in freedom, resist human control, and act each according to their own kind (39:5-18). God has given the wild ass its freedom and gave it the wilderness for a home. Similarly, the wild

²⁵at the trumpet's call he cries,
    "Aha!"
Even from afar he scents the battle,
    the roar of the officers and the
    shouting.
²⁶Is it by your understanding that
    the hawk soars,
    that he spreads his wings
    toward the south?
²⁷Does the eagle fly up at your com-
    mand
    to build his nest up high?
²⁸On a cliff he dwells and spends
    the night,
    on the spur of cliff or fortress.

²⁹From there he watches for his
    food;
    his eyes behold it afar off.
³⁰His young ones greedily drink
    blood;
    where the slain are, there is he.

40 ¹The LORD then answered Job and
    said:

²Will one who argues with the Al-
    mighty be corrected?
    Let him who would instruct
    God give answer!

³Then Job answered the LORD and
    said:

---

ox cannot be bound with rope or domesticated to suit Job. Only the ostrich is subject to divine control, for the Creator has withheld wisdom from her. Yet even this ungainly animal is alive, "swift of foot," and "makes sport" of horse and rider; the ostrich is free and wondrous (39:18). The horse, too, is powerful and fearless, racing on the plains and into battle, while the eagle and the hawk elude human discernment and control (39:19-30).

God's depiction of the animals is one of pure delight in their variety, strength, and prowess. Job is a know-nothing in this arena. He cannot fathom the ways of his fellow creatures, in their assortment and inscrutability, and their freedom to grow and flourish in their dwelling places. In this first speech, God has expanded horizons of the debate from Job's suffering to the glories of the created world, a world characterized by beauty and energy of life.

Has God been bullying Job? Surely divine interrogation is terrifying and overwhelming. At the same time, God brings Job into a new frame of reference within which to view his own plight and to consider the way God relates to the world. Chapter 40 continues God's speech for two verses and ends with an intimidating question and a challenge that seems to say that God will brook no criticism from a "faultfinder" like Job.

40:3-5 Job's first response

Uncharacteristically, Job responds to God's speech by silencing himself. He announces that he is "of little account," a lightweight who has no answer to these many questions. Has he been cowed by an intimidating, interrogating God, or does his silence signify something further. Has he finally come to a place of wonder where he can step back and contemplate

⁴Look, I am of little account; what
can I answer you?
I put my hand over my mouth.
⁵I have spoken once, I will not reply;
twice, but I will do so no more.

⁶Then the LORD answered Job out of
the storm and said:

⁷Gird up your loins now, like a
man.
I will question you, and you tell
me the answers!
⁸Would you refuse to acknowledge
my right?
Would you condemn me that
you may be justified?
⁹Have you an arm like that of God,
or can you thunder with a voice
like his?
¹⁰Adorn yourself with grandeur
and majesty,
and clothe yourself with glory
and splendor.
¹¹Let loose the fury of your wrath;
look at everyone who is proud
and bring them down.

¹²Look at everyone who is proud,
and humble them.
Tear down the wicked in their
place,
¹³bury them in the dust together;
in the hidden world imprison
them.
¹⁴Then will I too praise you,
for your own right hand can
save you.
¹⁵Look at Behemoth, whom I made
along with you,
who feeds on grass like an ox.
¹⁶See the strength in his loins,
the power in the sinews of his
belly.
¹⁷He carries his tail like a cedar;
the sinews of his thighs are like
cables.
¹⁸His bones are like tubes of bronze;
his limbs are like iron rods.
¹⁹He is the first of God's ways,
only his maker can approach
him with a sword.
²⁰For the mountains bring him
produce,

the beauty that has passed before him? Does his silence mean that he has become contemplative and now has room to come to grips with what he has lost and has been lamenting for many chapters? Perhaps his silence opens him, at last, to hear a response and to reframe his own experience. But the book, in its ambiguities and gaps, leaves interpretation to the readers, providing few clues to settle our many questions. No stage direction accompanies these speeches.

40:6–41:26 Yahweh's second speech

God's second speech repeats the opening challenge of the first (38:3) and amplifies it by asking Job if he would condemn God in order to justify himself (40:8). Although this challenge is indeed daunting, it does reveal that God has been listening to Job's accusations. God treats Job as a serious challenger, proposing that if Job can bring justice upon the earth by the power of his arm and the terror of his glance, then God would acknowledge that Job could save himself (40:9-13). Job, however, has not sought equality

and all wild animals make sport
there.
²¹Under lotus trees he lies,
in coverts of the reedy swamp.
²²The lotus trees cover him with
their shade;
all about him are the poplars in
the wadi.
²³If the river grows violent, he is not
disturbed;
he is tranquil though the Jordan
surges about his mouth.
²⁴Who can capture him by his eyes,
or pierce his nose with a trap?
²⁵Can you lead Leviathan about
with a hook,
or tie down his tongue with a
rope?
²⁶Can you put a ring into his nose,
or pierce through his cheek with
a gaff?
²⁷Will he then plead with you, time
after time,
or address you with tender
words?
²⁸Will he make a covenant with you

that you may have him as a
slave forever?
²⁹Can you play with him, as with a
bird?
Can you tie him up for your
little girls?
³⁰Will the traders bargain for him?
Will the merchants divide him
up?
³¹Can you fill his hide with barbs,
or his head with fish spears?
³²Once you but lay a hand upon
him,
no need to recall any other
conflict!

41 ¹Whoever might vainly hope to
do so
need only see him to be over-
thrown.
²No one is fierce enough to arouse
him;
who then dares stand before me?
³Whoever has assailed me, I will
pay back—
Everything under the heavens is
mine.

---

with God or the acquisition of power. He has been driven, instead, by a desire to understand his predicament.

After hurling this contest at Job as if he were a serious claimant to divine power, God turns to two specific and extremely frightening animals to further interrogate him. The first creature, Behemoth, is a land monster (40:13-24), and the second, Leviathan, is a sea monster (40:25–41:26). Some interpreters think Behemoth and Leviathan represent the hippopotamus and the crocodile, but it is more likely that they are mythic creatures who symbolize primordial chaos that God overcame at the creation of the world. They may be examples of the wicked ones that God challenges Job to "tear down the wicked in their place" (40:12). But God's relationship with these creatures is not adversarial; it is full of boastful pride.

The first statement about Behemoth addresses Job directly and asserts Behemoth's creaturely equality with Job. "Look at Behemoth, whom I made along with you" (40:15). An animal of marshy waters, Behemoth is far stronger than Job, but both are creatures of God. Stiff-tailed and iron-boned,

⁴I need hardly mention his limbs,
  his strength, and the fitness of
    his equipment.
⁵Who can strip off his outer
    garment,
  or penetrate his double armor?
⁶Who can force open the doors of
    his face,
  close to his terrible teeth?
⁷Rows of scales are on his back,
  tightly sealed together;
⁸They are fitted so close to each
    other
  that no air can come between
    them;
⁹So joined to one another
  that they hold fast and cannot
    be parted.
¹⁰When he sneezes, light flashes
    forth;
  his eyes are like the eyelids of
    the dawn.
¹¹Out of his mouth go forth torches;
  sparks of fire leap forth.

¹²From his nostrils comes smoke
  as from a seething pot or bowl.
¹³His breath sets coals afire;
  a flame comes from his mouth.
¹⁴Strength abides in his neck,
  and power leaps before him.
¹⁵The folds of his flesh stick
    together,
  it is cast over him and
    immovable.
¹⁶His heart is cast as hard as stone;
  cast as the lower millstone.
¹⁷When he rises up, the gods are
    afraid;
  when he crashes down, they fall
    back.
¹⁸Should a sword reach him, it will
    not avail;
  nor will spear, dart, or javelin.
¹⁹He regards iron as chaff,
  and bronze as rotten wood.
²⁰No arrow will put him to flight;
  slingstones used against him are
    but straw.

Behemoth is wild, ferocious, and makes sport of other wild animals (40:20). He is not disturbed by turbulence, and no one can capture him in his idyllic domain that provides for all his needs. Job and he are equals in God's creation.

The Leviathan (40:26–41:26) is an even more fearsome creature. Job has already mentioned this monster twice: once, in his opening speech, when he wishes "those skilled at disturbing Leviathan" to curse the night of his conception (3:8), and again, when Job asks if he must be watched like the sea monster for being chaotic and uncontrollable (7:12). Now God brings that beast before Job for his reflection, perhaps as a kind of mirror. Again God brags about the power, strength, and awesome beauty of this creature. Again interpreters see here evidence of ancient Ugaritic creation myths where God does battle with chaos monsters. But although those traditions are probably present, they are greatly tamed in this speech, since a battle does not occur.

God asks Job if he can curb, tame, domesticate, or do battle with this creature (40:25-32). Job must answer God's question with a resounding "No!" He cannot control this creature, but neither does God claim to do so. Instead, God shifts from questioning Job to a stance of ebullient delight in the wondrous Leviathan (41:2-26). In the style of a hymn of praise, God

95

(Top) Behemoth (Job 40:15) is a mythic creature or a land monster like the hippopotamus. (Bottom) Leviathan (Job 40:25) is another mythic creature or a sea monster like the crocodile.

²¹Clubs he regards as straw;
    he laughs at the crash of the
        spear.
²²Under him are sharp pottery
        fragments,
    spreading a threshing sledge
        upon the mire.
²³He makes the depths boil like a pot;
    he makes the sea like a perfume
        bottle.
²⁴Behind him he leaves a shining
        path;
    you would think the deep had
        white hair.
²⁵Upon the earth there is none like
        him,
    he was made fearless.

²⁶He looks over all who are
        haughty,
    he is king over all proud beasts.

42 ¹Then Job answered the LORD and
said:

²I know that you can do all things, ▸
    and that no purpose of yours
        can be hindered.
³"Who is this who obscures counsel ▸
    with ignorance?"
I have spoken but did not under-
    stand;
    things too marvelous for me,
        which I did not know.
⁴"Listen, and I will speak;
I will question you, and you tell me
    the answers."

---

praises Leviathan's fierceness, his strong limbs, terrible teeth, scales on his back, fire from his nostrils, and his general imperviousness to attack. Even the "mighty" are afraid when this creature rises up from the sea (41:17). "Upon the earth there is none like him" and "he is king over all proud beasts" (41:26). Although Leviathan is a fierce, proud creature suited for combat, this poetry is not about warfare between God and the wild creature. It is about divine joy in this most intrepid and fearsome animal. God does not repress Leviathan and Behemoth nor act in hostility toward them. Instead, the Creator leaves them in their natural state, uncontrolled and free to be themselves, wild and beautiful.

Rather than waging war with the creatures or even with Job, God opens up before Job the panorama of creation in its energy, variety, and wild beauty. Surely Job would be in fear and awe before this display, yet something more than intimidation is at work here. In the midst of the storm, God draws Job's attention away from himself to the awesomeness of the cosmos and its residents, kin to him, fellow creatures, untamed, and following their own paths. Some scholars note the absence of human creatures from God's speeches, yet humans are present in Job who is the one whom God addresses. God shows Job a world of immense marvels and beauty. Job participates in this glorious world and is one with it. This changes everything.

42:1-6 Job's second response

Job's final response reveals that his experience in the storm satisfies him and transforms his life, even if his words leave interpreters in doubt.

⁵By hearsay I had heard of you,
  but now my eye has seen you.
⁶Therefore I disown what I have
    said,
  and repent in dust and ashes.

IX. Epilogue

Job's Restoration. ⁷And after the
LORD had spoken these words to Job, the
LORD said to Eliphaz the Temanite, "My

Although Job promised previously to remain silent, he speaks again, acknowledging God's sovereignty and unstoppable will (42:2). Humbly he declares his know-nothing status before the glories of God's unfathomable creation. And he testifies that his encounter with God has altered him, as if he has become happily content with the experience of mystery and made alive again.

Job used to know about God through the words of other people, "by hearsay," but now in a marvelous declaration, he claims, "my eye has seen you" (42:5). Such seeing may refer to a vision, a common means of revelation in the Old Testament, but surely it signifies more. Job evokes Jeremiah's famous passage where the new covenant will mean that people will no longer teach one another because "Everyone, from least to greatest, shall know me" (Jer 31:34). Job is no longer reliant upon the word of others to have connection with God. Now he knows God directly from his own experience. With his own eye, in his own body, he has met God face to face.

The last line of his response, however, complicates interpretation of Job's words. Traditionally translated, "Therefore I despise myself and repent in dust and ashes" (42:6), the verse actually allows for several translations. In the NABRE translation, Job disowns his words and repents even though he is a righteous man. Both translations create problems. The former leaves Job in self-hatred, a defeated man beaten down by God. The latter shows Job renouncing the truthful laments he has set before God, who, in turn, praises Job's speech in the epilogue (42:7). But the Hebrew word often translated "repent" can also mean "be comforted," or "regret." Other translations create different nuances. In one, Job retracts his words and "is comforted by dust and ashes." In another, Job "rejects" the "dust and ashes," meaning that Job has stopped grieving and gotten on with his life.

The ambiguities of this line resist oversimplification. In light of the book's puzzling structure and unresolved debate, it is likely that the ambiguity is deliberate, a means to invite readers to enter Job's experience and come to terms with it for themselves. Whereas many interpreters find the speeches in the storm to be marked by chaos that Job learns to accept, this commentary concentrates the beauty of both the language and events in the storm. The breath-taking attraction of God's creation draws Job in and

anger blazes against you and your two friends! You have not spoken rightly concerning me, as has my servant Job. ⁸So now take seven bulls and seven rams, and go to my servant Job, and sacrifice a burnt offering for yourselves, and let my servant Job pray for you. To him I will show favor, and not punish your folly, for you have not spoken rightly concerning me, as has my servant Job." ⁹Then Eliphaz the Temanite, and Bildad the Shuhite, and Zophar the Naamathite, went and did as the LORD had commanded them. The LORD showed favor to Job.

¹⁰The LORD also restored the prosperity of Job, after he had prayed for his friends; the LORD even gave to Job twice as much as he had before. ¹¹Then all his brothers and sisters came to him, and all his former acquaintances, and they dined with him in his house. They consoled and comforted him for all the evil the LORD had brought upon him, and each one gave him a piece of money and a gold ring.

¹²Thus the LORD blessed the later days of Job more than his earlier ones. Now he had fourteen thousand sheep, six thousand camels, a thousand yoke of oxen, and a thousand she-donkeys. ¹³He also had seven sons and three daughters: ¹⁴the first daughter he called Jemimah, the second Keziah, and the third Keren-happuch. ¹⁵In all the land no other women were as beautiful as the daughters of Job; and their father gave them an inheritance among their brothers.

¹⁶After this, Job lived a hundred and forty years; and he saw his children, his grandchildren, and even his great-grandchildren. ¹⁷Then Job died, old and full of years.

---

transforms him. The beauty of God and God's world allures, takes him outward from his suffering, and enables him to relinquish his imaginary position at the center of the world. Experience of beauty sharpens attentiveness, creates a contemplative spirit, provokes gratitude, and opens one to care for the world.

Job's long, angry laments have helped to heal him and opened him to the life-affirming greeting from God. However we deal with the many lingering puzzles of the book, its beauty points to the beauty of the Creator and summons readers to the possibility of encounter with God in any of life's circumstances.

EPILOGUE

Job 42:7-17

The book surprises readers again by returning in a short epilogue of ten verses to prose narrative. These verses not only resume the folktale genre of the prologue to form a narrative frame around the book, they also return to the worldview of the book's beginning. There coherent themes of cause and effect rule in contrast to the poetry where ambiguity, complexity, and contradiction dominate the debates. The epilogue adds further complications to the book, even as it provides a satisfying happy ending. It brings readers back to a life where the good are rewarded and the wicked punished, as if the anguishing debates about God and human suffering only lead back to the beginning, having achieved little. The epilogue divides into two scenes: Job and friends (42:7-9) and Job's new life (42:10-17).

42:7-9 Job and friends

The narrator connects the epilogue with the speeches in the storm by setting events immediately "after the Lord had spoken these words to Job" (42:7). In these verses, God finally grants what Job desired all along, vindication of his righteousness or, at least, of the righteousness of his speech. But this honoring of Job's words is indirect, for it occurs in speech addressed to Eliphaz and comes only after God rebukes the friends, for "You have not spoken rightly concerning me, as has my servant Job" (42:7). It is strange that God does not affirm Job's words in the storm nor affirm him directly here. It may be that when Job sees God with his eye his needs are met and there are no other requirements of healing gestures between them.

The epilogue does not re-impose the theology of the prologue completely. Although the epilogue rewards Job, the innocent one, God does not punish the friends, so the chain of cause and effect is broken. God sets in place dynamics for rebuilding the friendship that fell upon the rocks of their disputes about Job's suffering. God tells Eliphaz and his two friends to offer sacrifice and Job will pray for them. God will not punish them because of Job's prayer. Job's experience of God in the storm enables him to intercede on his friends' behalf, altering his relationship with them and effecting a renewal of community. Job, the victim, extends a gesture of reconciliation to his persecuting friends.

42:10-17 Job's new life

God does more than approve of Job's words. In the second scene, God rewards him with good things, returning once again to the theology of the prologue. Job never asked God for restoration of anything he had lost except for their relationship. Now that Job has seen God himself, God gives him double what he had before (42:10-12). Among the doublings, Job's community comes first. Friends and family gather around him, feast with him, present gifts, and offer genuine comfort, "for all the evil the Lord had brought upon him" (42:11). Then he receives doubled numbers of animals and material wealth to make him twice as rich as before.

It is probably mistaken to ask where this community has been all along, since folktales tell their stories for the sake of the narrated events rather than to raise unanswered questions. Similarly, the replication of his family of ten children in the same gender balance as before does not address what all parents know, that lost children can never be replaced by new ones. The new children signify, instead, that Job has a full life, replete with a large family. But even this blessing is in some ways altered from the prologue because Job's daughters are not only named, they are given an inheritance with their brothers. By naming the daughters, and even more strikingly, listing them among inheritors, Job acts in ways his culture would find suspect (but see Num 27:1-11). Here the daughter's inheritance underscores Job's vast wealth as sufficient to include them, and for modern readers, it suggests that Job is not bound by the usual constraints of his society.

Job, the blessed servant of Yahweh, has come full circle. Restored to health, wealth, and community, he lives to see his children's children and dies old and full of years. And his latter days were more blessed than the former (42:12). Is this as a reward for his innocence, or is it a case of God pouring forth grace upon the beloved?

CONCLUSION

The book of Job is too rich in meaning and metaphoric power and complex in literary structure and theological debate to be reduced to one interpretation. Here are some ways to reflect upon the book as a whole.

A dramatic process

From a literary perspective, the book of Job evokes experiences it is trying to express. The prologue positions readers as privileged interpreters, sympathizers with Job, because we know he is the innocent victim of a deal made in heaven. The seemingly endless debates between Job and his friends immerse us in Job's despair, the friends' frustration, and Job's rage at them and God. The book's spiraling, contradictory interchanges wear us down, as if it were designed to force us into the depth of the struggle, to wrestle with it, examine it from many sides, only to be surprised and unbalanced again by events in the whirlwind and epilogue.

Against Elihu's confident denial, God appears in the storm. With a literary beauty that replicates the beautiful wildness of creation itself, God draws Job and readers into a world beyond ourselves. There, no intellectual answers resolve the conflicting voices, but God and Job meet, and Job changes. Finally, we rest with Job in the epilogue, a rest foreshadowed by the hymn to wisdom (ch. 28). Although Job lives happily ever after in peace, many questions remain because Job, the righteous one, receives rewards.

Rather than restating orthodoxy or hammering home one interpretive viewpoint, the book implies that the hymn to wisdom is a key to interpretation. Humans can do many things, but wisdom is hidden to everyone but God, a point the book illustrates. By leaving unanswered questions, the book provokes active participation in the drama of Job's life from its collapse to its restoration. Such participation is potentially transformative for readers.

Innocent suffering

Rather than explain why the innocent suffer, the book spreads a feast of understandings and theological positions about the matter. In telling of Job's life it presents injustice, life-stopping losses, grief, and the collapse of the worlds. This narrative is capable of embracing the sufferings of individuals and of whole peoples. Rich Job loses all to join the poor and outcast, symbolized by his place on the ash heap or garbage dump of his village. This broken figure reappears in the homeless, frightened refugees, displaced persons, and the hungry millions of our rich world. Job's suffering is undeserved, and his friends further isolate him in their inability to see him as he really is. The book calls readers to face our responses to the suffering around us, near and far, and to note the suffering, like Job, are God's favored.

By undermining easy interpretations of Job's plight, the text reminds readers of the limited grasp on truth of our theological positions. Repeatedly, through structural juxtapositions of conflicting parts and voices, the book displaces each voice, interpretation, and point of view regarding Job's suffering. Such unsettling argument summons us to openness to other understandings, to humility in holding our own truth, and to recognition that theologies and spiritualities change with new human circumstances. In times of uncertainty and meaninglessness, Job also calls us to stubborn fidelity to the God who transcends all reduction to rigid and narrow doctrine.

The prologue presents Job's disaster as a calculated design made in a heavenly bargain. Job suffers physically, mentally, and spiritually. His friends believe Job sinned and God merely responded by punishing him. Job thinks God betrayed him and, by extension, treats the world unjustly. When God speaks, it is to change the subject from Job's suffering to the beauty and wild freedom of creation. The book does not explain Job's suffering, nor does any text of the Bible settle the matter. Rather than explaining suffering, the New Testament presents another One who suffers innocently and whose suffering and death on the cross culminates in the gift of new life.

God humbles Job

Another way to view the same literary evidence is to understand the book as a divine put-down of Job. Some interpreters believe that when God changes the subject from Job's suffering to the creation, God disrespects and abuses Job who complains for legitimate reasons. In this view, divine interrogation in the storm emphasizes God's power and humiliates Job. The book, therefore, conceives of divine-human relationship as continuing combat. Job curses and God overpowers, bullies, and silences Job. Job's second response, in the traditional, although disputed, translation, "I despise myself and repent in dust and ashes" (NRSV, 42:6), expresses Job's diminishment. God's attempt to restore Job's life shows Job's charges against God are correct. In this interpretive approach, the book reinstates divine power and keeps humans humbled in the chaos of life.

Divine-human relationship

The book's primary concern, however, may not be the suffering of the innocent but the larger question of human relationship to God in the midst of suffering. Job's catastrophe provides the flesh and blood mess within which to debate the character of divine-human relationship. The Satan thinks divine-human relationship is a mercenary one. God buys human loyalty by giving gifts and putting a hedge of protection around Job. Job's words and actions in the prologue refute that point of view, for he remains utterly faithful. The Satan disappears from the book because his role in the story is finished. He lost his bet.

Job's friends reverse the Satan's perspective but are equally mechanistic. They insist that humans buy God's blessings or curses with their behavior. This theology of retribution gives humans controlling power over the actions of God. For both the friends and the Satan, divine-human relationships are one-sided arrangements. The Satan thinks God controls humans by giving or withholding good things. The friends think humans control God by loyalty or disloyalty. God has no choice but to bless or punish accordingly. Either way, divine-human relationship is compulsive and rule-driven.

Job breaks through these rigid patterns. In his experience, humans cannot control God, whom he finds to be both free and unreliable. He thinks God transcends human understanding, abides by no rules, and is inaccessible to humans. He thinks the sovereign God is beyond human capacity to understand and is also capricious and unjust. For him, God's being is deep mystery laced with cruelty.

When God appears, God not only affirms divine freedom, wildness, and beauty, but also the freedom and wild beauty of creation including Job. By implication, divine-human relationship is a mutual one where neither party controls the other, but both are free. In the epilogue, God approves Job's words. Is even Job's anger and despair about God's absence from the world evidence that Job has "spoken rightly" about God? (42:7). Are all Job's charges and accusations correct?

When God rejects the friends' words and declares Job to be right, the book appears to dismiss the friends' theology in the most authoritative way. But with great irony, the epilogue reinstates retribution. God blesses Job, the righteous one, and doubles all good things in his life. We are back where we started, but things are not the same.

Movement to mature faith

From another interpretative standpoint, Job's experiences resemble human struggles toward adult faith. As the story begins, Job is rich, secure, powerful, and surrounded by family and servants. Even when the Satan removes his blessings, he remains righteous. His piety is pre-critical and unquestioning, and his life has clarity of purpose, driven by acceptance and trust.

But in the poetry, Job's trust evaporates as rage, doubt, and despair displace it. The collapse of his life brings with it loss of the traditions that had supported him. Formerly, he was a comforter of others and a leader among them. After the breaking of his world, his theology no longer holds. It cannot explain, support, or illuminate his life. Instead, his life challenges his theology. Adding to his pain, no new way of understanding emerges except his assumption that God has betrayed him. He faces what later contemplatives might call the "dark night of the soul," when all support for faith unravels and one plunges into divine absence.

Yet in the process, Job remains faithful. He grows in power and rhetorical expansiveness. He laments what he has lost, voicing his anger and grief to his friends and to God. His truthful, angry speech becomes a vehicle of his loyalty. Job holds fast to his integrity despite efforts of his friends to talk him out of his experience of the world. It enables him to dare to challenge God and to demand that God step forward and explain matters to him.

Job's life propels him from a faith of few challenges into a chaotic spiral of doubt where faith no longer has any buttress or external support. Yet in the midst of bitter strife, he never lets go of God. Instead, he cries and yells angrily at God, telling his truth and keeping their relationship alive. When Job and God meet in the storm, Job knows a "reorientation," a new way of being that exceeds doctrinal or philosophical answers. His encounter with the beauty of divine revelation, of the cosmos, and by implication, the beauty of God, provide him with direct spiritual experience and a sense of oneness with all life. He shares life with the Behemoth, the Leviathan—proud and joyous expressions of divine life. In the storm, Job glimpses a world energized by the creative power of God.

That glimpse of the absolute wondrousness of the Creator and of creation reorders his relationships. His communal life becomes more open, inclusive, and peaceful. He repairs friendships, interceding on behalf of his friends and extending extraordinary care to his daughters. In the storm, Job receives a life-affirming greeting from another world, and however we deal with the book's many lingering questions, its beauty calls us to glimpse God's amazing creativity divinely loosed in the cosmos. It summons us to care for creation and all its inhabitants, especially those who know Job's suffering and abysmal pain. It urges us toward lives of worshipful gratitude.

REVIEW AIDS AND DISCUSSION TOPICS

Introduction *(pages 5–8)*

1. What explains the somewhat choppy structure of the book of Job? Why does the book contain both poetry and prose?

2. How should we approach the poetry in Job?

3. What is a lament? Read Psalm 69 as another example. What are its characteristics?

4. How might the community focus of Job's culture explain the concern of Job's friends over his situation?

5. What are the two values associated with Job's culture that are important in understanding his suffering?

1:1–2:13 Prologue *(pages 9–15)*

1. What kind of man is Job?

2. Who is "the Satan"? How is he different from our current concept of Satan? Does this difference matter? Why or why not?

3. What are Job's losses in the Satan's first attack? What is his response?

4. What is the second attack on Job? What is Job's response?

5. How do his friends behave when they first arrive on the scene?

4:1–14:22 First Round of Speeches *(pages 15–39)*

1. Why does the author of this commentary claim that the friends' speeches deepen Job's pain?

2. What are the complaints in Job's first lament? Do his words surprise you? Do we only think about suffering when we ourselves or others who are close to us are suffering?

3. Reading Eliphaz's first speech, find an example of the "theology of retribution." Does this apply to Job's case?

4. What is Eliphaz's judgment of Job and advice to him? Is it understandable after hearing Job's speech in chapter 3?

5. Do we still tend to see people who suffer as "responsible" for their suffering, even when we don't know the circumstances? Why?

6. What is Job's response? Is it likely to convince Eliphaz that he is wrong?

7. Are you surprised by Job's response? Does it make you think less of him? Do you think it is allowable for a righteous person to vent despair to God in this way?

8. How does Zophar's tone differ from that of Eliphaz and Bildad?

9. What is the ancient Hebrew understanding of the afterlife? How does that impact our understanding of Job's wish never to have been born?

15:1–21:34 Second Round of Speeches *(pages 39–53)*

1. How do the three speeches in this section elaborate the friends' criticism of Job?

2. How does Job respond?

3. From whom does Job seek justice?

4. In what way does Job's reply to Zophar reverse their theology of retribution?

22:1–31:37 Third Round of Speeches *(pages 54–74)*

1. What is unusual about this set of speeches? How do scholars explain the inconsistencies in composition and their role in the book?

2. Eliphaz seems even more entrenched in his beliefs about Job than he was in his first speech. Why?

3. What poetic devices does Job use in his reply?

4. Bildad's speech is also more pointed and single-minded than his others. What does he make clear here?

5. In chapter 28, Job suddenly turns from his complaint and remembers his past. What does this add to our understanding of Job?

6. The author of this commentary calls chapters 28–30 "Job's self-defense" case, ending with his demand that "God name the charges against him." Are you moved by his case? Do you think his friends would be?

7. Do you find Job's oaths convincing? What makes this a convincing form of argument?

32:1–37:24 Elihu Speaks *(pages 74–83)*

1. Who is Elihu? What is his character like?

2. What points does Elihu add to the arguments of the other three friends?

38:1–42:6 The Speeches in the Storm *(pages 83–98)*

1. What is God's answer to Job? Do you find it satisfactory?

2. Does Job's vow of silence mean he was wrong to lament? What else can it mean?

3. What is the purpose of introducing the Leviathan and the Behemoth?

4. Why do you think the experience of the storm is enough to settle Job's heart about what has happened to him?

42:7-17 The Epilogue *(pages 98–100)*

1. Does the epilogue supply a satisfying ending to the book of Job?

2. Do you think the friends should have been punished? Why aren't they?

3. Is Job's life fully restored? What has changed?

Conclusion *(pages 100–104)*

1. Read the five interpretations offered for reflection in this section of the commentary. Which is most satisfying for you?

2. What does the book of Job tell us about the divine-human relationship?

3. What does the book of Job tell us about community and individual suffering?

4. What does the book of Job tell us about the place of God in suffering?

5. What does the book of Job tell us about faith?

6. What are other possible interpretations of Job you'd like to explore?

INDEX OF CITATIONS FROM THE
CATECHISM OF THE CATHOLIC CHURCH

The arabic number(s) following the citation refer(s) to the paragraph number(s) in the *Catechism of the Catholic Church*.